Moments of Vision

Thomas Hardy

Table of Contents

Table of Contents

Moments of Vision

Table of Contents

Table of Contents

Table of Contents

Moments of Vision

Thomas Hardy

Moments of Vision

Moments of Vision

- AT A COUNTRY FAIR
- THE MEMORIAL BRASS: 186–
- HER LOVE–BIRDS
- PAYING CALLS
- THE UPPER BIRCH–LEAVES
- "IT NEVER LOOKS LIKE SUMMER"
- EVERYTHING COMES
- THE MAN WITH A PAST
- HE FEARS HIS GOOD FORTUNE
- HE WONDERS ABOUT HIMSELF
- JUBILATE
- HE REVISITS HIS FIRST SCHOOL
- "I THOUGHT, MY HEART"
- FRAGMENT
- MIDNIGHT ON THE GREAT WESTERN
- HONEYMOON TIME AT AN INN
- THE ROBIN
- "I ROSE AND WENT TO ROU'TOR TOWN"
- THE NETTLES
- IN A WAITING–ROOM
- THE CLOCK–WINDER
- OLD EXCURSIONS
- THE MASKED FACE
- IN A WHISPERING GALLERY
- THE SOMETHING THAT SAVED HIM
- THE ENEMY'S PORTRAIT
- IMAGININGS
- ON THE DOORSTEP
- SIGNS AND TOKENS
- PATHS OF FORMER TIME
- THE CLOCK OF THE YEARS
- AT THE PIANO
- THE SHADOW ON THE STONE
- IN THE GARDEN
- THE TREE AND THE LADY
- AN UPBRAIDING

MOMENTS OF VISION AND MISCELLANEOUS VERSES
by Thomas Hardy

MOMENTS OF VISION

That mirror
Which makes of men a transparency,
Who holds that mirror
And bids us such a breast–bare spectacle see
Of you and me?

That mirror
Whose magic penetrates like a dart,
Who lifts that mirror
And throws our mind back on us, and our heart,
Until we start?

That mirror
Works well in these night hours of ache;
Why in that mirror
Are tincts we never see ourselves once take
When the world is awake?

That mirror
Can test each mortal when unaware;
Yea, that strange mirror
May catch his last thoughts, whole life foul or fair,
Glassing it—where?

THE VOICE OF THINGS

Forty Augusts—aye, and several more—ago,
    When I paced the headlands loosed from dull employ,
The waves huzza'd like a multitude below
    In the sway of an all–including joy
      Without cloy.

Blankly I walked there a double decade after,
    When thwarts had flung their toils in front of me,
And I heard the waters wagging in a long ironic laughter
    At the lot of men, and all the vapoury
      Things that be.

Wheeling change has set me again standing where
    Once I heard the waves huzza at Lammas–tide;
But they supplicate now—like a congregation there
    Who murmur the Confession—I outside,
      Prayer denied.

"WHY BE AT PAINS?"

(Wooer's Song)

Why be at pains that I should know
     You sought not me?
Do breezes, then, make features glow
     So rosily?
Come, the lit port is at our back,
     And the tumbling sea;
Elsewhere the lampless uphill track
     To uncertainty!

O should not we two waifs join hands?
     I am alone,
You would enrich me more than lands
     By being my own.
Yet, though this facile moment flies,
     Close is your tone,
And ere to–morrow's dewfall dries
     I plough the unknown.

"WE SAT AT THE WINDOW"

(Bournemouth, 1875)

We sat at the window looking out,
And the rain came down like silken strings
That Swithin's day. Each gutter and spout
Babbled unchecked in the busy way
     Of witless things:

Nothing to read, nothing to see
Seemed in that room for her and me
      On Swithin's day.

We were irked by the scene, by our own selves; yes,
For I did not know, nor did she infer
How much there was to read and guess
By her in me, and to see and crown
      By me in her.
Wasted were two souls in their prime,
And great was the waste, that July time
      When the rain came down.

AFTERNOON SERVICE AT MELLSTOCK

(Circa 1850)

On afternoons of drowsy calm
      We stood in the panelled pew,
Singing one–voiced a Tate–and–Brady psalm
      To the tune of "Cambridge New."

We watched the elms, we watched the rooks,
      The clouds upon the breeze,
Between the whiles of glancing at our books,
      And swaying like the trees.

So mindless were those outpourings! –
      Though I am not aware

9

That I have gained by subtle thought on things
    Since we stood psalming there.

AT THE WICKET–GATE

There floated the sounds of church–chiming,
    But no one was nigh,
Till there came, as a break in the loneness,
    Her father, she, I.
And we slowly moved on to the wicket,
    And downlooking stood,
Till anon people passed, and amid them
    We parted for good.

Greater, wiser, may part there than we three
    Who parted there then,
But never will Fates colder–featured
    Hold sway there again.
Of the churchgoers through the still meadows
    No single one knew
What a play was played under their eyes there
    As thence we withdrew.

IN A MUSEUM

I

Here's the mould of a musical bird long passed from light,
Which over the earth before man came was winging;
There's a contralto voice I heard last night,
That lodges in me still with its sweet singing.

II

Such a dream is Time that the coo of this ancient bird
Has perished not, but is blent, or will be blending
Mid visionless wilds of space with the voice that I heard,
In the full—fugued song of the universe unending.

EXETER.

APOSTROPHE TO AN OLD PSALM TUNE

I met you first—ah, when did I first meet you?
When I was full of wonder, and innocent,
Standing meek—eyed with those of choric bent,
    While dimming day grew dimmer

Moments of Vision

In the pulpit–glimmer.

Much riper in years I met you—in a temple
Where summer sunset streamed upon our shapes,
And you spread over me like a gauze that drapes,
    And flapped from floor to rafters,
        Sweet as angels' laughters.

But you had been stripped of some of your old vesture
By Monk, or another. Now you wore no frill,
And at first you startled me. But I knew you still,
    Though I missed the minim's waver,
        And the dotted quaver.

I grew accustomed to you thus. And you hailed me
Through one who evoked you often. Then at last
Your raiser was borne off, and I mourned you had passed
    From my life with your late outsetter;
        Till I said, "'Tis better!"

But you waylaid me. I rose and went as a ghost goes,
And said, eyes–full "I'll never hear it again!
It is overmuch for scathed and memoried men
    When sitting among strange people
        Under their steeple."

Now, a new stirrer of tones calls you up before me
And wakes your speech, as she of Endor did
(When sought by Saul who, in disguises hid,
    Fell down on the earth to hear it)
        Samuel's spirit.

So, your quired oracles beat till they make me tremble
As I discern your mien in the old attire,
Here in these turmoiled years of belligerent fire
    Living still on—and onward, maybe,

Till Doom's great day be!

Sunday, August 13, 1916.

AT THE WORD "FAREWELL"

She looked like a bird from a cloud
      On the clammy lawn,
Moving alone, bare–browed
      In the dim of dawn.
The candles alight in the room
      For my parting meal
Made all things withoutdoors loom
      Strange, ghostly, unreal.

The hour itself was a ghost,
      And it seemed to me then
As of chances the chance furthermost
      I should see her again.
I beheld not where all was so fleet
      That a Plan of the past
Which had ruled us from birthtime to meet
      Was in working at last:

No prelude did I there perceive
      To a drama at all,
Or foreshadow what fortune might weave
      From beginnings so small;

But I rose as if quicked by a spur
      I was bound to obey,
And stepped through the casement to her
      Still alone in the gray.

"I am leaving you . . . Farewell!" I said,
      As I followed her on
By an alley bare boughs overspread;
      "I soon must be gone!"
Even then the scale might have been turned
      Against love by a feather,
– But crimson one cheek of hers burned
      When we came in together.

FIRST SIGHT OF HER AND AFTER

A day is drawing to its fall
      I had not dreamed to see;
The first of many to enthrall
      My spirit, will it be?
Or is this eve the end of all
      Such new delight for me?

I journey home: the pattern grows
      Of moonshades on the way:
"Soon the first quarter, I suppose,"
      Sky–glancing travellers say;
I realize that it, for those,

Has been a common day.

THE RIVAL

I determined to find out whose it was –
The portrait he looked at so, and sighed;
Bitterly have I rued my meanness
And wept for it since he died!

I searched his desk when he was away,
And there was the likeness—yes, my own!
Taken when I was the season's fairest,
And time–lines all unknown.

I smiled at my image, and put it back,
And he went on cherishing it, until
I was chafed that he loved not the me then living,
But that past woman still.

Well, such was my jealousy at last,
I destroyed that face of the former me;
Could you ever have dreamed the heart of woman
Would work so foolishly!

15

HEREDITY

I am the family face;
Flesh perishes, I live on,
Projecting trait and trace
Through time to times anon,
And leaping from place to place
Over oblivion.

The years—heired feature that can
In curve and voice and eye
Despise the human span
Of durance—that is I;
The eternal thing in man,
That heeds no call to die.

"YOU WERE THE SORT THAT MEN FORGET"

You were the sort that men forget;
Though I—not yet! –
Perhaps not ever. Your slighted weakness
Adds to the strength of my regret!

You'd not the art—you never had

For good or bad –
To make men see how sweet your meaning,
Which, visible, had charmed them glad.

You would, by words inept let fall,
Offend them all,
Even if they saw your warm devotion
Would hold your life's blood at their call.

You lacked the eye to understand
Those friends offhand
Whose mode was crude, though whose dim purport
Outpriced the courtesies of the bland.

I am now the only being who
Remembers you
It may be. What a waste that Nature
Grudged soul so dear the art its due!

SHE, I, AND THEY

I was sitting,
She was knitting,
And the portraits of our fore–folk hung around;
When there struck on us a sigh;
"Ah—what is that?" said I:
"Was it not you?" said she. "A sigh did sound."

17

I had not breathed it,
Nor the night–wind heaved it,
And how it came to us we could not guess;
And we looked up at each face
Framed and glazed there in its place,
Still hearkening; but thenceforth was silentness.

Half in dreaming,
"Then its meaning,"
Said we, "must be surely this; that they repine
That we should be the last
Of stocks once unsurpassed,
And unable to keep up their sturdy line."

1916.

NEAR LANIVET, 1872

There was a stunted handpost just on the crest,
Only a few feet high:
She was tired, and we stopped in the twilight–time for her rest,
At the crossways close thereby.

She leant back, being so weary, against its stem,
And laid her arms on its own,
Each open palm stretched out to each end of them,
Her sad face sideways thrown.

Moments of Vision

Her white–clothed form at this dim–lit cease of day
    Made her look as one crucified
In my gaze at her from the midst of the dusty way,
    And hurriedly "Don't," I cried.

I do not think she heard. Loosing thence she said,
    As she stepped forth ready to go,
"I am rested now.—Something strange came into my head;
    I wish I had not leant so!"

And wordless we moved onward down from the hill
    In the west cloud's murked obscure,
And looking back we could see the handpost still
    In the solitude of the moor.

"It struck her too," I thought, for as if afraid
    She heavily breathed as we trailed;
Till she said, "I did not think how 'twould look in the shade,
    When I leant there like one nailed."

I, lightly: "There's nothing in it. For YOU, anyhow!"
—"O I know there is not," said she . . .
"Yet I wonder . . . If no one is bodily crucified now,
    In spirit one may be!"

And we dragged on and on, while we seemed to see
    In the running of Time's far glass
Her crucified, as she had wondered if she might be
    Some day.—Alas, alas!

JOYS OF MEMORY

When the spring comes round, and a certain day
Looks out from the brume by the eastern copsetrees
And says, Remember,
I begin again, as if it were new,
A day of like date I once lived through,
Whiling it hour by hour away;
So shall I do till my December,
When spring comes round.

I take my holiday then and my rest
Away from the dun life here about me,
Old hours re–greeting
With the quiet sense that bring they must
Such throbs as at first, till I house with dust,
And in the numbness my heartsome zest
For things that were, be past repeating
When spring comes round.

TO THE MOON

"What have you looked at, Moon,
In your time,

Now long past your prime?"
"O, I have looked at, often looked at
      Sweet, sublime,
Sore things, shudderful, night and noon
      In my time."

"What have you mused on, Moon,
      In your day,
    So aloof, so far away?"
"O, I have mused on, often mused on
      Growth, decay,
Nations alive, dead, mad, aswoon,
      In my day!"

"Have you much wondered, Moon,
      On your rounds,
    Self—wrapt, beyond Earth's bounds?"
"Yea, I have wondered, often wondered
      At the sounds
Reaching me of the human tune
      On my rounds."

"What do you think of it, Moon,
      As you go?
    Is Life much, or no?"
"O, I think of it, often think of it
      As a show
God ought surely to shut up soon,
      As I go."

COPYING ARCHITECTURE IN AN OLD MINSTER

(Wimborne)

How smartly the quarters of the hour march by
  That the jack–o'–clock never forgets;
 Ding–dong; and before I have traced a cusp's eye,
Or got the true twist of the ogee over,
   A double ding–dong ricochetts.

Just so did he clang here before I came,
  And so will he clang when I'm gone
 Through the Minster's cavernous hollows—the same
Tale of hours never more to be will he deliver
  To the speechless midnight and dawn!

I grow to conceive it a call to ghosts,
  Whose mould lies below and around.
 Yes; the next "Come, come," draws them out from their posts,
And they gather, and one shade appears, and another,
  As the eve–damps creep from the ground.

See—a Courtenay stands by his quatre–foiled tomb,
  And a Duke and his Duchess near;
 And one Sir Edmund in columned gloom,
And a Saxon king by the presbytery chamber;
  And shapes unknown in the rear.

Maybe they have met for a parle on some plan
  To better ail–stricken mankind;
 I catch their cheepings, though thinner than
The overhead creak of a passager's pinion

When leaving land behind.

Or perhaps they speak to the yet unborn,
    And caution them not to come
To a world so ancient and trouble–torn,
Of foiled intents, vain lovingkindness,
    And ardours chilled and numb.

They waste to fog as I stir and stand,
    And move from the arched recess,
And pick up the drawing that slipped from my hand,
And feel for the pencil I dropped in the cranny
    In a moment's forgetfulness.

TO SHAKESPEARE

AFTER THREE HUNDRED YEARS

    Bright baffling Soul, least capturable of themes,
    Thou, who display'dst a life of common–place,
    Leaving no intimate word or personal trace
    Of high design outside the artistry
        Of thy penned dreams,
Still shalt remain at heart unread eternally.

    Through human orbits thy discourse to–day,
    Despite thy formal pilgrimage, throbs on
    In harmonies that cow Oblivion,
    And, like the wind, with all–uncared effect

Moments of Vision

        Maintain a sway
Not fore–desired, in tracks unchosen and unchecked.

       And yet, at thy last breath, with mindless note
       The borough clocks but samely tongued the hour,
       The Avon just as always glassed the tower,
       Thy age was published on thy passing–bell
           But in due rote
With other dwellers' deaths accorded a like knell.

       And at the strokes some townsman (met, maybe,
       And thereon queried by some squire's good dame
       Driving in shopward) may have given thy name,
       With, "Yes, a worthy man and well–to–do;
           Though, as for me,
I knew him but by just a neighbour's nod, 'tis true.

       "I' faith, few knew him much here, save by word,
       He having elsewhere led his busier life;
       Though to be sure he left with us his wife."
—"Ah, one of the tradesmen's sons, I now recall . . .
           Witty, I've heard . . .
We did not know him . . . Well, good–day. Death comes to all."

       So, like a strange bright bird we sometimes find
       To mingle with the barn–door brood awhile,
       Then vanish from their homely domicile –
       Into man's poesy, we wot not whence,
           Flew thy strange mind,
Lodged there a radiant guest, and sped for ever thence.

1916.

QUID HIC AGIS?

I

When I weekly knew
An ancient pew,
And murmured there
The forms of prayer
And thanks and praise
In the ancient ways,
And heard read out
During August drought
That chapter from Kings
Harvest–time brings;
– How the prophet, broken
By griefs unspoken,
Went heavily away
To fast and to pray,
And, while waiting to die,
The Lord passed by,
And a whirlwind and fire
Drew nigher and nigher,
And a small voice anon
Bade him up and be gone, –
I did not apprehend
As I sat to the end
And watched for her smile
Across the sunned aisle,
That this tale of a seer
Which came once a year
Might, when sands were heaping,

Moments of Vision

Be like a sweat creeping,
Or in any degree
Bear on her or on me!

II

When later, by chance
Of circumstance,
It befel me to read
On a hot afternoon
At the lectern there
The selfsame words
As the lesson decreed,
To the gathered few
From the hamlets near –
Folk of flocks and herds
Sitting half aswoon,
Who listened thereto
As women and men
Not overmuch
Concerned at such –
So, like them then,
I did not see
What drought might be
With me, with her,
As the Kalendar
Moved on, and Time
Devoured our prime.

III

But now, at last,
When our glory has passed,
And there is no smile
From her in the aisle,
But where it once shone

A marble, men say,
With her name thereon
Is discerned to–day;
And spiritless
In the wilderness
I shrink from sight
And desire the night,
(Though, as in old wise,
I might still arise,
Go forth, and stand
And prophesy in the land),
I feel the shake
Of wind and earthquake,
And consuming fire
Nigher and nigher,
And the voice catch clear,
"What doest thou here?"

The Spectator 1916. During the War.

ON A MIDSUMMER EVE

I idly cut a parsley stalk,
And blew therein towards the moon;
I had not thought what ghosts would walk
With shivering footsteps to my tune.

I went, and knelt, and scooped my hand

As if to drink, into the brook,
And a faint figure seemed to stand
Above me, with the bygone look.

I lipped rough rhymes of chance, not choice,
I thought not what my words might be;
There came into my ear a voice
That turned a tenderer verse for me.

TIMING HER

(Written to an old folk–tune)

Lalage's coming:
Where is she now, O?
Turning to bow, O,
And smile, is she,
Just at parting,
Parting, parting,
As she is starting
To come to me?

Where is she now, O,
Now, and now, O,
Shadowing a bough, O,
Of hedge or tree
As she is rushing,
Rushing, rushing,
Gossamers brushing

28

Moments of Vision

To come to me?

Lalage's coming;
Where is she now, O;
Climbing the brow, O,
Of hills I see?
Yes, she is nearing,
Nearing, nearing,
Weather unfearing
To come to me.

Near is she now, O,
Now, and now, O;
Milk the rich cow, O,
Forward the tea;
Shake the down bed for her,
Linen sheets spread for her,
Drape round the head for her
Coming to me.

Lalage's coming,
She's nearer now, O,
End anyhow, O,
To—day's husbandry!
Would a gilt chair were mine,
Slippers of vair were mine,
Brushes for hair were mine
Of ivory!

What will she think, O,
She who's so comely,
Viewing how homely
A sort are we!
Nothing resplendent,
No prompt attendant,
Not one dependent

29

Pertaining to me!

Lalage's coming;
Where is she now, O?
Fain I'd avow, O,
Full honestly
Nought here's enough for her,
All is too rough for her,
Even my love for her
Poor in degree.

She's nearer now, O,
Still nearer now, O,
She 'tis, I vow, O,
Passing the lea.
Rush down to meet her there,
Call out and greet her there,
Never a sweeter there
Crossed to me!

Lalage's come; aye,
Come is she now, O! . . .
Does Heaven allow, O,
A meeting to be?
Yes, she is here now,
Here now, here now,
Nothing to fear now,
Here's Lalage!

BEFORE KNOWLEDGE

When I walked roseless tracks and wide,
Ere dawned your date for meeting me,
O why did you not cry Halloo
Across the stretch between, and say:

"We move, while years as yet divide,
On closing lines which—though it be
You know me not nor I know you –
Will intersect and join some day!"

Then well I had borne
Each scraping thorn;
But the winters froze,
And grew no rose;
No bridge bestrode
The gap at all;
No shape you showed,
And I heard no call!

THE BLINDED BIRD

So zestfully canst thou sing?
And all this indignity,
With God's consent, on thee!
Blinded ere yet a–wing

By the red—hot needle thou,
I stand and wonder how
So zestfully thou canst sing!

Resenting not such wrong,
Thy grievous pain forgot,
Eternal dark thy lot,
Groping thy whole life long;
After that stab of fire;
Enjailed in pitiless wire;
Resenting not such wrong!

Who hath charity? This bird.
Who suffereth long and is kind,
Is not provoked, though blind
And alive ensepulchred?
Who hopeth, endureth all things?
Who thinketh no evil, but sings?
Who is divine? This bird.

"THE WIND BLEW WORDS"

The wind blew words along the skies,
    And these it blew to me
Through the wide dusk: "Lift up your eyes,
    Behold this troubled tree,
Complaining as it sways and plies;
    It is a limb of thee.

"Yea, too, the creatures sheltering round –
      Dumb figures, wild and tame,
Yea, too, thy fellows who abound –
      Either of speech the same
Or far and strange—black, dwarfed, and browned,
      They are stuff of thy own frame."

I moved on in a surging awe
      Of inarticulateness
At the pathetic Me I saw
      In all his huge distress,
Making self–slaughter of the law
      To kill, break, or suppress.

THE FADED FACE

How was this I did not see
Such a look as here was shown
Ere its womanhood had blown
Past its first felicity? –
That I did not know you young,
      Faded Face,
         Know you young!

Why did Time so ill bestead
That I heard no voice of yours
Hail from out the curved contours

Of those lips when rosy red;
Weeted not the songs they sung,
        Faded Face,
                Songs they sung!

By these blanchings, blooms of old,
And the relics of your voice –
Leavings rare of rich and choice
From your early tone and mould –
Let me mourn,—aye, sorrow–wrung,
        Faded Face,
                Sorrow–wrung!

THE RIDDLE

I

Stretching eyes west
Over the sea,
Wind foul or fair,
Always stood she
Prospect–impressed;
Solely out there
Did her gaze rest,
Never elsewhere
Seemed charm to be.

II

Always eyes east
Ponders she now –
As in devotion –
Hills of blank brow
Where no waves plough.
Never the least
Room for emotion
Drawn from the ocean
Does she allow.

THE DUEL

"I am here to time, you see;
The glade is well–screened—eh?—against alarm;
Fit place to vindicate by my arm
The honour of my spotless wife,
Who scorns your libel upon her life
In boasting intimacy!

"'All hush–offerings you'll spurn,
My husband. Two must come; one only go,'
She said. 'That he'll be you I know;
To faith like ours Heaven will be just,
And I shall abide in fullest trust
Your speedy glad return.'"

"Good. Here am also I;

And we'll proceed without more waste of words
    To warm your cockpit. Of the swords
    Take you your choice. I shall thereby
    Feel that on me no blame can lie,
        Whatever Fate accords."

    So stripped they there, and fought,
And the swords clicked and scraped, and the onsets sped;
    Till the husband fell; and his shirt was red
    With streams from his heart's hot cistern. Nought
    Could save him now; and the other, wrought
        Maybe to pity, said:

    "Why did you urge on this?
Your wife assured you; and 't had better been
    That you had let things pass, serene
    In confidence of long–tried bliss,
    Holding there could be nought amiss
        In what my words might mean."

    Then, seeing nor ruth nor rage
Could move his foeman more—now Death's deaf thrall –
    He wiped his steel, and, with a call
    Like turtledove to dove, swift broke
    Into the copse, where under an oak
        His horse cropt, held by a page.

    "All's over, Sweet," he cried
To the wife, thus guised; for the young page was she.
    "'Tis as we hoped and said 't would be.
    He never guessed . . . We mount and ride
    To where our love can reign uneyed.
        He's clay, and we are free."

AT MAYFAIR LODGINGS

How could I be aware,
The opposite window eyeing
As I lay listless there,
That through its blinds was dying
One I had rated rare
Before I had set me sighing
For another more fair?

Had the house—front been glass,
My vision unobscuring,
Could aught have come to pass
More happiness—insuring
To her, loved as a lass
When spouseless, all—alluring?
I reckon not, alas!

So, the square window stood,
Steadily night—long shining
In my close neighbourhood,
Who looked forth undivining
That soon would go for good
One there in pain reclining,
Unpardoned, unadieu'd.

Silently screened from view
Her tragedy was ending
That need not have come due
Had she been less unbending.
How near, near were we two

At that last vital rending, –
And neither of us knew!

TO MY FATHER'S VIOLIN

Does he want you down there
In the Nether Glooms where
The hours may be a dragging load upon him,
As he hears the axle grind
Round and round
Of the great world, in the blind
Still profound
Of the night–time? He might liven at the sound
Of your string, revealing you had not forgone him.

In the gallery west the nave,
But a few yards from his grave,
Did you, tucked beneath his chin, to his bowing
Guide the homely harmony
Of the quire
Who for long years strenuously –
Son and sire –
Caught the strains that at his fingering low or higher
From your four thin threads and eff–holes came outflowing.

And, too, what merry tunes
He would bow at nights or noons
That chanced to find him bent to lute a measure,

When he made you speak his heart
      As in dream,
Without book or music—chart,
      On some theme
Elusive as a jack—o'—lanthorn's gleam,
And the psalm of duty shelved for trill of pleasure.

      Well, you can not, alas,
      The barrier overpass
That screens him in those Mournful Meads hereunder,
      Where no fiddling can be heard
         In the glades
      Of silentness, no bird
         Thrills the shades;
Where no viol is touched for songs or serenades,
No bowing wakes a congregation's wonder.

      He must do without you now,
      Stir you no more anyhow
To yearning concords taught you in your glory;
      While, your strings a tangled wreck,
         Once smart drawn,
      Ten worm—wounds in your neck,
         Purflings wan
With dust—hoar, here alone I sadly con
Your present dumbness, shape your olden story.

1916.

THE STATUE OF LIBERTY

Moments of Vision

This statue of Liberty, busy man,
    Here erect in the city square,
I have watched while your scrubbings, this early morning,
      Strangely wistful,
      And half tristful,
    Have turned her from foul to fair;

With your bucket of water, and mop, and brush,
    Bringing her out of the grime
That has smeared her during the smokes of winter
      With such glumness
      In her dumbness,
    And aged her before her time.

You have washed her down with motherly care –
    Head, shoulders, arm, and foot,
To the very hem of the robes that drape her –
      All expertly
      And alertly,
    Till a long stream, black with soot,

Flows over the pavement to the road,
    And her shape looms pure as snow:
I read you are hired by the City guardians –
      May be yearly,
      Or once merely –
    To treat the statues so?

"Oh, I'm not hired by the Councilmen
    To cleanse the statues here.
I do this one as a self–willed duty,
      Not as paid to,
      Or at all made to,

But because the doing is dear."

Ah, then I hail you brother and friend!
  Liberty's knight divine.
What you have done would have been my doing,
   Yea, most verily,
   Well, and thoroughly,
  Had but your courage been mine!

"Oh I care not for Liberty's mould,
  Liberty charms not me;
What's Freedom but an idler's vision,
   Vain, pernicious,
   Often vicious,
  Of things that cannot be!

"Memory it is that brings me to this –
  Of a daughter—my one sweet own.
She grew a famous carver's model,
   One of the fairest
   And of the rarest:–
  She sat for the figure as shown.

"But alas, she died in this distant place
  Before I was warned to betake
Myself to her side! . . . And in love of my darling,
   In love of the fame of her,
   And the good name of her,
  I do this for her sake."

Answer I gave not. Of that form
  The carver was I at his side;
His child, my model, held so saintly,
   Grand in feature,
   Gross in nature,
  In the dens of vice had died.

41

THE BACKGROUND AND THE FIGURE

(Lover's Ditty)

I think of the slope where the rabbits fed,
 Of the periwinks' rockwork lair,
Of the fuchsias ringing their bells of red –
 And the something else seen there.

Between the blooms where the sod basked bright,
 By the bobbing fuchsia trees,
Was another and yet more eyesome sight –
 The sight that richened these.

I shall seek those beauties in the spring,
 When the days are fit and fair,
But only as foils to the one more thing
 That also will flower there!

THE CHANGE

Moments of Vision

Out of the past there rises a week –
      Who shall read the years O! –
Out of the past there rises a week
      Enringed with a purple zone.
Out of the past there rises a week
When thoughts were strung too thick to speak,
And the magic of its lineaments remains with me alone.

In that week there was heard a singing –
      Who shall spell the years, the years! –
In that week there was heard a singing,
      And the white owl wondered why.
In that week, yea, a voice was ringing,
And forth from the casement were candles flinging
Radiance that fell on the deodar and lit up the path thereby.

Could that song have a mocking note? –
      Who shall unroll the years O! –
Could that song have a mocking note
      To the white owl's sense as it fell?
Could that song have a mocking note
As it trilled out warm from the singer's throat,
And who was the mocker and who the mocked when two felt all was well?

In a tedious trampling crowd yet later –
      Who shall bare the years, the years! –
In a tedious trampling crowd yet later,
      When silvery singings were dumb;
In a crowd uncaring what time might fate her,
Mid murks of night I stood to await her,
And the twanging of iron wheels gave out the signal that she was
come.

She said with a travel–tired smile –
      Who shall lift the years O! –
She said with a travel–tired smile,

> Half scared by scene so strange;
> She said, outworn by mile on mile,
> The blurred lamps wanning her face the while,
"O Love, I am here; I am with you!" . . . Ah, that there should have
come a change!

> O the doom by someone spoken –
> > Who shall unseal the years, the years! –
> O the doom that gave no token,
> > When nothing of bale saw we:
> O the doom by someone spoken,
> O the heart by someone broken,
The heart whose sweet reverberances are all time leaves to me.

Jan.–Feb. 1913.

SITTING ON THE BRIDGE

(Echo of an old song)

> Sitting on the bridge
> Past the barracks, town and ridge,
At once the spirit seized us
To sing a song that pleased us –
As "The Fifth" were much in rumour;
It was "Whilst I'm in the humour,
> Take me, Paddy, will you now?"
> And a lancer soon drew nigh,
> And his Royal Irish eye

44

Said, "Willing, faith, am I,
O, to take you anyhow, dears,
To take you anyhow."

But, lo!—dad walking by,
Cried, "What, you lightheels! Fie!
Is this the way you roam
And mock the sunset gleam?"
And he marched us straightway home,
Though we said, "We are only, daddy,
Singing, 'Will you take me, Paddy?'"
—Well, we never saw from then
If we sang there anywhen,
The soldier dear again,
Except at night in dream–time,
Except at night in dream.

Perhaps that soldier's fighting
In a land that's far away,
Or he may be idly plighting
Some foreign hussy gay;
Or perhaps his bones are whiting
In the wind to their decay! . . .
Ah!—does he mind him how
The girls he saw that day
On the bridge, were sitting singing
At the time of curfew–ringing,
"Take me, Paddy; will you now, dear?
Paddy, will you now?"

GREY'S BRIDGE.

THE YOUNG CHURCHWARDEN

When he lit the candles there,
And the light fell on his hand,
And it trembled as he scanned
Her and me, his vanquished air
Hinted that his dream was done,
And I saw he had begun
     To understand.

When Love's viol was unstrung,
Sore I wished the hand that shook
Had been mine that shared her book
While that evening hymn was sung,
His the victor's, as he lit
Candles where he had bidden us sit
     With vanquished look.

Now her dust lies listless there,
His afar from tending hand,
What avails the victory scanned?
Does he smile from upper air:
"Ah, my friend, your dream is done;
And 'tis YOU who have begun
     To understand!

"I TRAVEL AS A PHANTOM NOW"

I travel as a phantom now,
For people do not wish to see
In flesh and blood so bare a bough
　　　As Nature makes of me.

And thus I visit bodiless
Strange gloomy households often at odds,
And wonder if Man's consciousness
　　　Was a mistake of God's.

And next I meet you, and I pause,
And think that if mistake it were,
As some have said, O then it was
　　　One that I well can bear!

1915.

LINES TO A MOVEMENT IN MOZART'S E–FLAT SYMPHONY

　　　Show me again the time
　　　When in the Junetide's prime

47

We flew by meads and mountains northerly! –
Yea, to such freshness, fairness, fulness, fineness, freeness,
    Love lures life on.

Show me again the day
    When from the sandy bay
We looked together upon the pestered sea! –
Yea, to such surging, swaying, sighing, swelling, shrinking,
    Love lures life on.

Show me again the hour
    When by the pinnacled tower
We eyed each other and feared futurity! –
Yea, to such bodings, broodings, beatings, blanchings, blessings,
    Love lures life on.

Show me again just this:
    The moment of that kiss
Away from the prancing folk, by the strawberry–tree! –
Yea, to such rashness, ratheness, rareness, ripeness, richness,
    Love lures life on.

Begun November 1898.

"IN THE SEVENTIES"

"Qui deridetur ab amico suo sicut ego."—JOB.

In the seventies I was bearing in my breast,
                    Penned tight,
Certain starry thoughts that threw a magic light
On the worktimes and the soundless hours of rest
In the seventies; aye, I bore them in my breast
                    Penned tight.

In the seventies when my neighbours—even my friend –
                    Saw me pass,
Heads were shaken, and I heard the words, "Alas,
For his onward years and name unless he mend!"
In the seventies, when my neighbours and my friend
                    Saw me pass.

In the seventies those who met me did not know
                    Of the vision
That immuned me from the chillings of mis–prision
And the damps that choked my goings to and fro
In the seventies; yea, those nodders did not know
                    Of the vision.

In the seventies nought could darken or destroy it,
                    Locked in me,
Though as delicate as lamp–worm's lucency;
Neither mist nor murk could weaken or alloy it
In the seventies!—could not darken or destroy it,
                    Locked in me.

THE PEDIGREE

Moments of Vision

I

I bent in the deep of night
Over a pedigree the chronicler gave
As mine; and as I bent there, half–unrobed,
The uncurtained panes of my window–square let in the watery light
Of the moon in its old age:
And green–rheumed clouds were hurrying past where mute and cold it globed
Like a drifting dolphin's eye seen through a lapping wave.

II

So, scanning my sire–sown tree,
And the hieroglyphs of this spouse tied to that,
With offspring mapped below in lineage,
Till the tangles troubled me,
The branches seemed to twist into a seared and cynic face
Which winked and tokened towards the window like a Mage
Enchanting me to gaze again thereat.

III

It was a mirror now,
And in it a long perspective I could trace
Of my begetters, dwindling backward each past each
All with the kindred look,
Whose names had since been inked down in their place
On the recorder's book,
Generation and generation of my mien, and build, and brow.

IV

And then did I divine

That every heave and coil and move I made
Within my brain, and in my mood and speech,
    Was in the glass portrayed
    As long forestalled by their so making it;
The first of them, the primest fuglemen of my line,
Being fogged in far antiqueness past surmise and reason's reach.

V

    Said I then, sunk in tone,
"I am merest mimicker and counterfeit! –
    Though thinking, I AM I
    AND WHAT I DO I DO MYSELF ALONE."
—The cynic twist of the page thereat unknit
Back to its normal figure, having wrought its purport wry,
    The Mage's mirror left the window–square,
And the stained moon and drift retook their places there.

1916.

THIS HEART; A WOMAN'S DREAM

    At midnight, in the room where he lay dead
    Whom in his life I had never clearly read,
I thought if I could peer into that citadel
    His heart, I should at last know full and well

What hereto had been known to him alone,

Moments of Vision

Despite our long sit—out of years foreflown,
"And if," I said, "I do this for his memory's sake,
    It would not wound him, even if he could wake."

So I bent over him. He seemed to smile
With a calm confidence the whole long while
That I, withdrawing his heart, held it and, bit by bit,
    Perused the unguessed things found written on it.

It was inscribed like a terrestrial sphere
With quaint vermiculations close and clear –
His graving. Had I known, would I have risked the stroke
    Its reading brought, and my own heart nigh broke!

Yes, there at last, eyes opened, did I see
His whole sincere symmetric history;
There were his truth, his simple singlemindedness,
    Strained, maybe, by time's storms, but there no less.

There were the daily deeds from sun to sun
In blindness, but good faith, that he had done;
There were regrets, at instances wherein he swerved
    (As he conceived) from cherishings I had deserved.

There were old hours all figured down as bliss –
Those spent with me—(how little had I thought this!)
There those when, at my absence, whether he slept or waked,
    (Though I knew not 'twas so!) his spirit ached.

There that when we were severed, how day dulled
Till time joined us anew, was chronicled:
And arguments and battlings in defence of me
    That heart recorded clearly and ruddily.

I put it back, and left him as he lay
While pierced the morning pink and then the gray

Into each dreary room and corridor around,
    Where I shall wait, but his step will not sound.

WHERE THEY LIVED

    Dishevelled leaves creep down
    Upon that bank to–day,
Some green, some yellow, and some pale brown;
    The wet bents bob and sway;
The once warm slippery turf is sodden
    Where we laughingly sat or lay.

    The summerhouse is gone,
    Leaving a weedy space;
The bushes that veiled it once have grown
    Gaunt trees that interlace,
Through whose lank limbs I see too clearly
    The nakedness of the place.

    And where were hills of blue,
    Blind drifts of vapour blow,
And the names of former dwellers few,
    If any, people know,
And instead of a voice that called, "Come in, Dears,"
    Time calls, "Pass below!"

THE OCCULTATION

When the cloud shut down on the morning shine,
    And darkened the sun,
I said, "So ended that joy of mine
    Years back begun."

But day continued its lustrous roll
    In upper air;
And did my late irradiate soul
    Live on somewhere?

LIFE LAUGHS ONWARD

Rambling I looked for an old abode
Where, years back, one had lived I knew;
Its site a dwelling duly showed,
    But it was new.

I went where, not so long ago,
The sod had riven two breasts asunder;
Daisies throve gaily there, as though
    No grave were under.

I walked along a terrace where
Loud children gambolled in the sun;
The figure that had once sat there
      Was missed by none.

Life laughed and moved on unsubdued,
I saw that Old succumbed to Young:
'Twas well. My too regretful mood
      Died on my tongue.

THE PEACE–OFFERING

It was but a little thing,
Yet I knew it meant to me
Ease from what had given a sting
To the very birdsinging
      Latterly.

But I would not welcome it;
And for all I then declined
O the regrettings infinite
When the night–processions flit
      Through the mind!

"SOMETHING TAPPED"

Something tapped on the pane of my room
      When there was never a trace
Of wind or rain, and I saw in the gloom
      My weary Beloved's face.

"O I am tired of waiting," she said,
      "Night, morn, noon, afternoon;
So cold it is in my lonely bed,
      And I thought you would join me soon!"

I rose and neared the window–glass,
      But vanished thence had she:
Only a pallid moth, alas,
      Tapped at the pane for me.

August 1913.

THE WOUND

I climbed to the crest,
      And, fog–festooned,
The sun lay west

56

Like a crimson wound:

Like that wound of mine
        Of which none knew,
For I'd given no sign
        That it pierced me through.

A MERRYMAKING IN QUESTION

"I will get a new string for my fiddle,
        And call to the neighbours to come,
And partners shall dance down the middle
        Until the old pewter—wares hum:
        And we'll sip the mead, cyder, and rum!"

From the night came the oddest of answers:
        A hollow wind, like a bassoon,
And headstones all ranged up as dancers,
        And cypresses droning a croon,
        And gurgoyles that mouthed to the tune.

"I SAID AND SANG HER EXCELLENCE"

(Fickle Lover's Song)

Moments of Vision

I said and sang her excellence:
　　　They called it laud undue.
　　　　　(Have your way, my heart, O!)
Yet what was homage far above
The plain deserts of my olden Love
　　　Proved verity of my new.

"She moves a sylph in picture–land,
　　　Where nothing frosts the air:"
　　　　　(Have your way, my heart, O!)
"To all winged pipers overhead
She is known by shape and song," I said,
　　　Conscious of licence there.

I sang of her in a dim old hall
　　　Dream–built too fancifully,
　　　　　(Have your way, my heart, O!)
But lo, the ripe months chanced to lead
My feet to such a hall indeed,
　　　Where stood the very She.

Strange, startling, was it then to learn
　　　I had glanced down unborn time,
　　　　　(Have your way, my heart, O!)
And prophesied, whereby I knew
That which the years had planned to do
　　　In warranty of my rhyme.

BY RUSHY–POND.

58

A JANUARY NIGHT

(1879)

The rain smites more and more,
The east wind snarls and sneezes;
Through the joints of the quivering door
     The water wheezes.

The tip of each ivy–shoot
Writhes on its neighbour's face;
There is some hid dread afoot
     That we cannot trace.

Is it the spirit astray
Of the man at the house below
Whose coffin they took in to–day?
     We do not know.

A KISS

By a wall the stranger now calls his,
Was born of old a particular kiss,
Without forethought in its genesis;
Which in a trice took wing on the air.

And where that spot is nothing shows:
      There ivy calmly grows,
      And no one knows
      What a birth was there!

That kiss is gone where none can tell –
Not even those who felt its spell:
It cannot have died; that know we well.
Somewhere it pursues its flight,
One of a long procession of sounds
      Travelling aethereal rounds
      Far from earth's bounds
      In the infinite.

THE ANNOUNCEMENT

They came, the brothers, and took two chairs
      In their usual quiet way;
And for a time we did not think
      They had much to say.

And they began and talked awhile
      Of ordinary things,
Till spread that silence in the room
      A pent thought brings.

And then they said: "The end has come.
      Yes: it has come at last."

And we looked down, and knew that day
      A spirit had passed.

THE OXEN

Christmas Eve, and twelve of the clock.
      "Now they are all on their knees,"
An elder said as we sat in a flock
      By the embers in hearthside ease.

We pictured the meek mild creatures where
      They dwelt in their strawy pen,
Nor did it occur to one of us there
      To doubt they were kneeling then.

So fair a fancy few would weave
      In these years! Yet, I feel,
If someone said on Christmas Eve,
      "Come; see the oxen kneel

"In the lonely barton by yonder coomb
      Our childhood used to know,"
I should go with him in the gloom,
      Hoping it might be so.

1915.

61

THE TRESSES

"When the air was damp
It made my curls hang slack
As they kissed my neck and back
While I footed the salt-aired track
I loved to tramp.

"When it was dry
They would roll up crisp and tight
As I went on in the light
Of the sun, which my own sprite
Seemed to outvie.

"Now I am old;
And have not one gay curl
As I had when a girl
For dampness to unfurl
Or sun uphold!"

THE PHOTOGRAPH

The flame crept up the portrait line by line
As it lay on the coals in the silence of night's profound,
        And over the arm's incline,
And along the marge of the silkwork superfine,
And gnawed at the delicate bosom's defenceless round.

Then I vented a cry of hurt, and averted my eyes;
The spectacle was one that I could not bear,
        To my deep and sad surprise;
But, compelled to heed, I again looked furtive-wise
Till the flame had eaten her breasts, and mouth, and hair.

"Thank God, she is out of it now!" I said at last,
In a great relief of heart when the thing was done
        That had set my soul aghast,
And nothing was left of the picture unsheathed from the past
But the ashen ghost of the card it had figured on.

She was a woman long hid amid packs of years,
She might have been living or dead; she was lost to my sight,
        And the deed that had nigh drawn tears
Was done in a casual clearance of life's arrears;
But I felt as if I had put her to death that night! . . .

* * *

– Well; she knew nothing thereof did she survive,
And suffered nothing if numbered among the dead;
        Yet—yet—if on earth alive
Did she feel a smart, and with vague strange anguish strive?
If in heaven, did she smile at me sadly and shake her head?

ON A HEATH

I could hear a gown–skirt rustling
    Before I could see her shape,
Rustling through the heather
    That wove the common's drape,
On that evening of dark weather
    When I hearkened, lips agape.

And the town–shine in the distance
    Did but baffle here the sight,
And then a voice flew forward:
    Dear, is't you? I fear the night!"
And the herons flapped to norward
    In the firs upon my right.

There was another looming
    Whose life we did not see;
There was one stilly blooming
    Full nigh to where walked we;
There was a shade entombing
    All that was bright of me.

AN ANNIVERSARY

It was at the very date to which we have come,
    In the month of the matching name,
When, at a like minute, the sun had upswum,
    Its couch–time at night being the same.
And the same path stretched here that people now follow,
    And the same stile crossed their way,
And beyond the same green hillock and hollow
    The same horizon lay;
And the same man pilgrims now hereby who pilgrimed here that day.

Let so much be said of the date–day's sameness;
    But the tree that neighbours the track,
And stoops like a pedlar afflicted with lameness,
    Knew of no sogged wound or windcrack.
And the joints of that wall were not enshrouded
    With mosses of many tones,
And the garth up afar was not overcrowded
    With a multitude of white stones,
And the man's eyes then were not so sunk that you saw the socket–
bones.

KINGSTON–MAURWARD EWELEASE.

"BY THE RUNIC STONE"

(Two who became a story)

By the Runic Stone

They sat, where the grass sloped down,
And chattered, he white–hatted, she in brown,
Pink–faced, breeze–blown.

Rapt there alone
In the transport of talking so
In such a place, there was nothing to let them know
What hours had flown.

And the die thrown
By them heedlessly there, the dent
It was to cut in their encompassment,
Were, too, unknown.

It might have strown
Their zest with qualms to see,
As in a glass, Time toss their history
From zone to zone!

THE PINK FROCK

"O my pretty pink frock,
I sha'n't be able to wear it!
Why is he dying just now?
I hardly can bear it!

"He might have contrived to live on;
But they say there's no hope whatever:

And must I shut myself up,
    And go out never?

"O my pretty pink frock,
Puff—sleeved and accordion—pleated!
He might have passed in July,
    And not so cheated!"

TRANSFORMATIONS

Portion of this yew
Is a man my grandsire knew,
Bosomed here at its foot:
This branch may be his wife,
A ruddy human life
Now turned to a green shoot.

These grasses must be made
Of her who often prayed,
Last century, for repose;
And the fair girl long ago
Whom I often tried to know
May be entering this rose.

So, they are not underground,
But as nerves and veins abound
In the growths of upper air,
And they feel the sun and rain,

And the energy again
That made them what they were!

IN HER PRECINCTS

Her house looked cold from the foggy lea,
And the square of each window a dull black blur
      Where showed no stir:
Yes, her gloom within at the lack of me
Seemed matching mine at the lack of her.

The black squares grew to be squares of light
As the eyeshade swathed the house and lawn,
      And viols gave tone;
There was glee within. And I found that night
The gloom of severance mine alone.

KINGSTON–MAURWARD PARK.

THE LAST SIGNAL

(Oct. 11, 1886)
A MEMORY OF WILLIAM BARNES

Silently I footed by an uphill road
That led from my abode to a spot yew–boughed;
Yellowly the sun sloped low down to westward,
And dark was the east with cloud.

Then, amid the shadow of that livid sad east,
Where the light was least, and a gate stood wide,
Something flashed the fire of the sun that was facing it,
Like a brief blaze on that side.

Looking hard and harder I knew what it meant –
The sudden shine sent from the livid east scene;
It meant the west mirrored by the coffin of my friend there,
Turning to the road from his green,

To take his last journey forth—he who in his prime
Trudged so many a time from that gate athwart the land!
Thus a farewell to me he signalled on his grave–way,
As with a wave of his hand.

WINTERBORNE–CAME PATH.

THE HOUSE OF SILENCE

"That is a quiet place –
That house in the trees with the shady lawn."

"—If, child, you knew what there goes on
You would not call it a quiet place.
Why, a phantom abides there, the last of its race,
      And a brain spins there till dawn."

      "But I see nobody there, –
Nobody moves about the green,
Or wanders the heavy trees between."
"—Ah, that's because you do not bear
The visioning powers of souls who dare
      To pierce the material screen.

      "Morning, noon, and night,
Mid those funereal shades that seem
The uncanny scenery of a dream,
Figures dance to a mind with sight,
And music and laughter like floods of light
      Make all the precincts gleam.

      "It is a poet's bower,
Through which there pass, in fleet arrays,
Long teams of all the years and days,
Of joys and sorrows, of earth and heaven,
That meet mankind in its ages seven,
      An aion in an hour."

GREAT THINGS

Moments of Vision

Sweet cyder is a great thing,
    A great thing to me,
Spinning down to Weymouth town
    By Ridgway thirstily,
And maid and mistress summoning
    Who tend the hostelry:
O cyder is a great thing,
    A great thing to me!

The dance it is a great thing,
    A great thing to me,
With candles lit and partners fit
    For night–long revelry;
And going home when day–dawning
    Peeps pale upon the lea:
O dancing is a great thing,
    A great thing to me!

Love is, yea, a great thing,
    A great thing to me,
When, having drawn across the lawn
    In darkness silently,
A figure flits like one a–wing
    Out from the nearest tree:
O love is, yes, a great thing,
    A great thing to me!

Will these be always great things,
    Great things to me? . . .
Let it befall that One will call,
    "Soul, I have need of thee:"
What then? Joy–jaunts, impassioned flings,
    Love, and its ecstasy,
Will always have been great things,
    Great things to me!

THE CHIMES

That morning when I trod the town
The twitching chimes of long renown
    Played out to me
The sweet Sicilian sailors' tune,
And I knew not if late or soon
    My day would be:

A day of sunshine beryl—bright
And windless; yea, think as I might,
    I could not say,
Even to within years' measure, when
One would be at my side who then
    Was far away.

When hard utilitarian times
Had stilled the sweet Saint—Peter's chimes
    I learnt to see
That bale may spring where blisses are,
And one desired might be afar
    Though near to me.

THE FIGURE IN THE SCENE

It pleased her to step in front and sit
    Where the cragged slope was green,
While I stood back that I might pencil it
    With her amid the scene;
      Till it gloomed and rained;
But I kept on, despite the drifting wet
    That fell and stained
My draught, leaving for curious quizzings yet
    The blots engrained.

And thus I drew her there alone,
    Seated amid the gauze
Of moisture, hooded, only her outline shown,
    With rainfall marked across.
      —Soon passed our stay;
Yet her rainy form is the Genius still of the spot,
    Immutable, yea,
Though the place now knows her no more, and has known her not
    Ever since that day.

From an old note.

"WHY DID I SKETCH"

Why did I sketch an upland green,
      And put the figure in
      Of one on the spot with me? –
For now that one has ceased to be seen
      The picture waxes akin
      To a wordless irony.

If you go drawing on down or cliff
      Let no soft curves intrude
      Of a woman's silhouette,
But show the escarpments stark and stiff
      As in utter solitude;
      So shall you half forget.

Let me sooner pass from sight of the sky
      Than again on a thoughtless day
      Limn, laugh, and sing, and rhyme
With a woman sitting near, whom I
      Paint in for love, and who may
      Be called hence in my time!

From an old note.

CONJECTURE

If there were in my kalendar

No Emma, Florence, Mary,
What would be my existence now –
    A hermit's?—wanderer's weary? –
        How should I live, and how
        Near would be death, or far?

Could it have been that other eyes
        Might have uplit my highway?
That fond, sad, retrospective sight
        Would catch from this dim byway
            Prized figures different quite
            From those that now arise?

With how strange aspect would there creep
        The dawn, the night, the daytime,
If memory were not what it is
        In song–time, toil, or pray–time. –
            O were it else than this,
            I'd pass to pulseless sleep!

THE BLOW

That no man schemed it is my hope –
Yea, that it fell by will and scope
        Of That Which some enthrone,
And for whose meaning myriads grope.

For I would not that of my kind

There should, of his unbiassed mind,
    Have been one known
Who such a stroke could have designed;

Since it would augur works and ways
Below the lowest that man assays
    To have hurled that stone
Into the sunshine of our days!

And if it prove that no man did,
And that the Inscrutable, the Hid,
    Was cause alone
Of this foul crash our lives amid,

I'll go in due time, and forget
In some deep graveyard's oubliette
    The thing whereof I groan,
And cease from troubling; thankful yet

Time's finger should have stretched to show
No aimful author's was the blow
    That swept us prone,
But the Immanent Doer's That doth not know,

Which in some age unguessed of us
May lift Its blinding incubus,
    And see, and own:
"It grieves me I did thus and thus!"

LOVE THE MONOPOLIST

Moments of Vision

(Young Lover's Reverie)

The train draws forth from the station–yard,
    And with it carries me.
I rise, and stretch out, and regard
    The platform left, and see
An airy slim blue form there standing,
    And know that it is she.

While with strained vision I watch on,
    The figure turns round quite
To greet friends gaily; then is gone . . .
    The import may be slight,
But why remained she not hard gazing
    Till I was out of sight?

"O do not chat with others there,"
    I brood. "They are not I.
O strain your thoughts as if they were
    Gold bands between us; eye
All neighbour scenes as so much blankness
    Till I again am by!

"A troubled soughing in the breeze
    And the sky overhead
Let yourself feel; and shadeful trees,
    Ripe corn, and apples red,
Read as things barren and distasteful
    While we are separated!

"When I come back uncloak your gloom,
    And let in lovely day;
Then the long dark as of the tomb
    Can well be thrust away

77

With sweet things I shall have to practise,
        And you will have to say!"

Begun 1871: finished –

AT MIDDLE–FIELD GATE IN FEBRUARY

The bars are thick with drops that show
        As they gather themselves from the fog
Like silver buttons ranged in a row,
And as evenly spaced as if measured, although
        They fall at the feeblest jog.

They load the leafless hedge hard by,
        And the blades of last year's grass,
While the fallow ploughland turned up nigh
In raw rolls, clammy and clogging lie –
        Too clogging for feet to pass.

How dry it was on a far–back day
        When straws hung the hedge and around,
When amid the sheaves in amorous play
In curtained bonnets and light array
        Bloomed a bevy now underground!

BOCKHAMPTON LANE.

THE YOUTH WHO CARRIED A LIGHT

I saw him pass as the new day dawned,
    Murmuring some musical phrase;
Horses were drinking and floundering in the pond,
    And the tired stars thinned their gaze;
Yet these were not the spectacles at all that he conned,
    But an inner one, giving out rays.

Such was the thing in his eye, walking there,
    The very and visible thing,
A close light, displacing the gray of the morning air,
    And the tokens that the dark was taking wing;
And was it not the radiance of a purpose rare
    That might ripe to its accomplishing?

What became of that light? I wonder still its fate!
    Was it quenched ere its full apogee?
Did it struggle frail and frailer to a beam emaciate?
    Did it thrive till matured in verity?
Or did it travel on, to be a new young dreamer's freight,
    And thence on infinitely?

1915.

THE HEAD ABOVE THE FOG

Something do I see
Above the fog that sheets the mead,
A figure like to life indeed,
Moving along with spectre–speed,
    Seen by none but me.

O the vision keen! –
Tripping along to me for love
As in the flesh it used to move,
Only its hat and plume above
    The evening fog–fleece seen.

In the day–fall wan,
When nighted birds break off their song,
Mere ghostly head it skims along,
Just as it did when warm and strong,
    Body seeming gone.

Such it is I see
Above the fog that sheets the mead –
Yea, that which once could breathe and plead! –
Skimming along with spectre–speed
    To a last tryst with me.

OVERLOOKING THE RIVER STOUR

The swallows flew in the curves of an eight
      Above the river–gleam
      In the wet June's last beam:
Like little crossbows animate
The swallows flew in the curves of an eight
      Above the river–gleam.

Planing up shavings of crystal spray
      A moor–hen darted out
      From the bank thereabout,
And through the stream–shine ripped his way;
Planing up shavings of crystal spray
      A moor–hen darted out.

Closed were the kingcups; and the mead
      Dripped in monotonous green,
      Though the day's morning sheen
Had shown it golden and honeybee'd;
Closed were the kingcups; and the mead
      Dripped in monotonous green.

And never I turned my head, alack,
      While these things met my gaze
      Through the pane's drop–drenched glaze,
To see the more behind my back . . .
O never I turned, but let, alack,
      These less things hold my gaze!

THE MUSICAL BOX

Lifelong to be
Seemed the fair colour of the time;
That there was standing shadowed near
A spirit who sang to the gentle chime
Of the self—struck notes, I did not hear,
I did not see.

Thus did it sing
To the mindless lyre that played indoors
As she came to listen for me without:
"O value what the nonce outpours –
This best of life—that shines about
Your welcoming!"

I had slowed along
After the torrid hours were done,
Though still the posts and walls and road
Flung back their sense of the hot—faced sun,
And had walked by Stourside Mill, where broad
Stream—lilies throng.

And I descried
The dusky house that stood apart,
And her, white—muslined, waiting there
In the porch with high—expectant heart,
While still the thin mechanic air
Went on inside.

At whiles would flit
Swart bats, whose wings, be–webbed and tanned,
Whirred like the wheels of ancient clocks:
She laughed a hailing as she scanned
Me in the gloom, the tuneful box
  Intoning it.

  Lifelong to be
I thought it. That there watched hard by
A spirit who sang to the indoor tune,
"O make the most of what is nigh!"
I did not hear in my dull soul–swoon –
  I did not see.

ON STURMINSTER FOOT–BRIDGE

(ONOMATOPOEIC)

Reticulations creep upon the slack stream's face
  When the wind skims irritably past,
The current clucks smartly into each hollow place
That years of flood have scrabbled in the pier's sodden base;
  The floating–lily leaves rot fast.

On a roof stand the swallows ranged in wistful waiting rows,
  Till they arrow off and drop like stones
Among the eyot–withies at whose foot the river flows;
And beneath the roof is she who in the dark world shows

As a lattice–gleam when midnight moans.

ROYAL SPONSORS

"The king and the queen will stand to the child;
  'Twill be handed down in song;
And it's no more than their deserving,
With my lord so faithful at Court so long,
   And so staunch and strong.

"O never before was known such a thing!
  'Twill be a grand time for all;
And the beef will be a whole–roast bullock,
And the servants will have a feast in the hall,
   And the ladies a ball.

"While from Jordan's stream by a traveller,
  In a flagon of silver wrought,
And by caravan, stage–coach, wain, and waggon
A precious trickle has been brought,
   Clear as when caught."

The morning came. To the park of the peer
  The royal couple bore;
And the font was filled with the Jordan water,
And the household awaited their guests before
   The carpeted door.

But when they went to the silk–lined cot
    The child was found to have died.
"What's now to be done? We can disappoint not
The king and queen!" the family cried
    With eyes spread wide.

"Even now they approach the chestnut–drive!
    The service must be read."
"Well, since we can't christen the child alive,
By God we shall have to christen him dead!"
    The marquis said.

Thus, breath–forsaken, a corpse was taken
    To the private chapel—yea –
And the king knew not, nor the queen, God wot,
That they answered for one returned to clay
    At the font that day.

OLD FURNITURE

I know not how it may be with others
    Who sit amid relics of householdry
That date from the days of their mothers' mothers,
    But well I know how it is with me
    Continually.

I see the hands of the generations
    That owned each shiny familiar thing

Moments of Vision

In play on its knobs and indentations,
    And with its ancient fashioning
        Still dallying:

Hands behind hands, growing paler and paler,
    As in a mirror a candle–flame
Shows images of itself, each frailer
    As it recedes, though the eye may frame
        Its shape the same.

On the clock's dull dial a foggy finger,
    Moving to set the minutes right
With tentative touches that lift and linger
    In the wont of a moth on a summer night,
        Creeps to my sight.

On this old viol, too, fingers are dancing –
    As whilom—just over the strings by the nut,
The tip of a bow receding, advancing
    In airy quivers, as if it would cut
        The plaintive gut.

And I see a face by that box for tinder,
    Glowing forth in fits from the dark,
And fading again, as the linten cinder
    Kindles to red at the flinty spark,
        Or goes out stark.

Well, well. It is best to be up and doing,
    The world has no use for one to–day
Who eyes things thus—no aim pursuing!
    He should not continue in this stay,
        But sink away.

A THOUGHT IN TWO MOODS

I saw it—pink and white—revealed
    Upon the white and green;
The white and green was a daisied field,
    The pink and white Ethleen.

And as I looked it seemed in kind
    That difference they had none;
The two fair bodiments combined
    As varied miens of one.

A sense that, in some mouldering year,
    As one they both would lie,
Made me move quickly on to her
    To pass the pale thought by.

She laughed and said: "Out there, to me,
    You looked so weather–browned,
And brown in clothes, you seemed to be
    Made of the dusty ground!"

THE LAST PERFORMANCE

"I am playing my oldest tunes," declared she,
　　　"All the old tunes I know, –
Those I learnt ever so long ago."
– Why she should think just then she'd play them
　　　Silence cloaks like snow.

When I returned from the town at nightfall
　　　Notes continued to pour
As when I had left two hours before:
It's the very last time," she said in closing;
　　　"From now I play no more."

A few morns onward found her fading,
　　　And, as her life outflew,
I thought of her playing her tunes right through;
And I felt she had known of what was coming,
　　　And wondered how she knew.

1912.

"YOU ON THE TOWER"

I

"You on the tower of my factory –
　　　What do you see up there?
Do you see Enjoyment with wide wings
　　　Advancing to reach me here?"

– "Yea; I see Enjoyment with wide wings
      Advancing to reach you here."

II

"Good. Soon I'll come and ask you
      To tell me again thereon . . .
Well, what is he doing now? Hoi, there!"
—"He still is flying on."
"Ah, waiting till I have full–finished.
      Good. Tell me again anon . . .

III

Hoi, Watchman! I'm here. When comes he?
      Between my sweats I am chill."
—"Oh, you there, working still?
Why, surely he reached you a time back,
      And took you miles from your mill?
He duly came in his winging,
      And now he has passed out of view.
How can it be that you missed him?
      He brushed you by as he flew."

THE INTERLOPER

"And I saw the figure and visage of Madness seeking for a home."

89

Moments of Vision

There are three folk driving in a quaint old chaise,
And the cliff–side track looks green and fair;
I view them talking in quiet glee
As they drop down towards the puffins' lair
By the roughest of ways;
But another with the three rides on, I see,
      Whom I like not to be there!

No: it's not anybody you think of. Next
A dwelling appears by a slow sweet stream
Where two sit happy and half in the dark:
They read, helped out by a frail–wick'd gleam,
Some rhythmic text;
But one sits with them whom they don't mark,
      One I'm wishing could not be there.

No: not whom you knew and name. And now
I discern gay diners in a mansion–place,
And the guests dropping wit—pert, prim, or choice,
And the hostess's tender and laughing face,
And the host's bland brow;
I cannot help hearing a hollow voice,
      And I'd fain not hear it there.

No: it's not from the stranger you met once. Ah,
Yet a goodlier scene than that succeeds;
People on a lawn—quite a crowd of them. Yes,
And they chatter and ramble as fancy leads;
And they say, "Hurrah!"
To a blithe speech made; save one, mirthless,
      Who ought not to be there.

Nay: it's not the pale Form your imagings raise,
That waits on us all at a destined time,
It is not the Fourth Figure the Furnace showed,
O that it were such a shape sublime;

In these latter days!
It is that under which best lives corrode;
      Would, would it could not be there!

LOGS ON THE HEARTH

A MEMORY OF A SISTER

      The fire advances along the log
          Of the tree we felled,
Which bloomed and bore striped apples by the peck
        Till its last hour of bearing knelled.

      The fork that first my hand would reach
          And then my foot
In climbings upward inch by inch, lies now
        Sawn, sapless, darkening with soot.

      Where the bark chars is where, one year,
          It was pruned, and bled –
Then overgrew the wound. But now, at last,
        Its growings all have stagnated.

      My fellow–climber rises dim
          From her chilly grave –
Just as she was, her foot near mine on the bending limb,
        Laughing, her young brown hand awave.

December 1915.

THE SUNSHADE

Ah—it's the skeleton of a lady's sunshade,
    Here at my feet in the hard rock's chink,
    Merely a naked sheaf of wires! –
    Twenty years have gone with their livers and diers
    Since it was silked in its white or pink.

Noonshine riddles the ribs of the sunshade,
    No more a screen from the weakest ray;
    Nothing to tell us the hue of its dyes,
    Nothing but rusty bones as it lies
    In its coffin of stone, unseen till to–day.

Where is the woman who carried that sun–shade
    Up and down this seaside place? –
    Little thumb standing against its stem,
    Thoughts perhaps bent on a love–stratagem,
    Softening yet more the already soft face!

Is the fair woman who carried that sunshade
    A skeleton just as her property is,
    Laid in the chink that none may scan?
    And does she regret—if regret dust can –
    The vain things thought when she flourished this?

SWANAGE CLIFFS.

THE AGEING HOUSE

When the walls were red
That now are seen
To be overspread
With a mouldy green,
A fresh fair head
Would often lean
From the sunny casement
And scan the scene,
While blithely spoke the wind to the little sycamore tree.

But storms have raged
Those walls about,
And the head has aged
That once looked out;
And zest is suaged
And trust is doubt,
And slow effacement
Is rife throughout,
While fiercely girds the wind at the long–limbed sycamore tree!

THE CAGED GOLDFINCH

Within a churchyard, on a recent grave,
    I saw a little cage
That jailed a goldfinch. All was silence save
    Its hops from stage to stage.

There was inquiry in its wistful eye,
    And once it tried to sing;
Of him or her who placed it there, and why,
    No one knew anything.

AT MADAME TUSSAUD'S IN VICTORIAN YEARS

"That same first fiddler who leads the orchestra to−night
    Here fiddled four decades of years ago;
He bears the same babe−like smile of self−centred delight,
Same trinket on watch−chain, same ring on the hand with the bow.

"But his face, if regarded, is woefully wanner, and drier,
    And his once dark beard has grown straggling and gray;
Yet a blissful existence he seems to have led with his lyre,
In a trance of his own, where no wearing or tearing had sway.

"Mid these wax figures, who nothing can do, it may seem
      That to do but a little thing counts a great deal;
To be watched by kings, councillors, queens, may be flattering to him
—
With their glass eyes longing they too could wake notes that appeal."

* * *

Ah, but he played staunchly—that fiddler—whoever he was,
      With the innocent heart and the soul–touching string:
May he find the Fair Haven! For did he not smile with good cause?
Yes; gamuts that graced forty years'–flight were not a small thing!

THE BALLET

They crush together—a rustling heap of flesh –
Of more than flesh, a heap of souls; and then
      They part, enmesh,
    And crush together again,
Like the pink petals of a too sanguine rose
      Frightened shut just when it blows.

Though all alike in their tinsel livery,
And indistinguishable at a sweeping glance,
      They muster, maybe,
    As lives wide in irrelevance;
A world of her own has each one underneath,
      Detached as a sword from its sheath.

Daughters, wives, mistresses; honest or false, sold, bought;
Hearts of all sizes; gay, fond, gushing, or penned,
                    Various in thought
                    Of lover, rival, friend;
Links in a one–pulsed chain, all showing one smile,
                    Yet severed so many a mile!

THE FIVE STUDENTS

        The sparrow dips in his wheel–rut bath,
            The sun grows passionate–eyed,
    And boils the dew to smoke by the paddock–path;
            As strenuously we stride, –
Five of us; dark He, fair He, dark She, fair She, I,
            All beating by.

        The air is shaken, the high–road hot,
            Shadowless swoons the day,
    The greens are sobered and cattle at rest; but not
            We on our urgent way, –
Four of us; fair She, dark She, fair He, I, are there,
            But one—elsewhere.

        Autumn moulds the hard fruit mellow,
            And forward still we press
    Through moors, briar–meshed plantations, clay–pits yellow,
            As in the spring hours—yes,

Three of us: fair He, fair She, I, as heretofore,
        But—fallen one more.

The leaf drops: earthworms draw it in
        At night–time noiselessly,
The fingers of birch and beech are skeleton–thin,
        And yet on the beat are we, –
Two of us; fair She, I. But no more left to go
        The track we know.

Icicles tag the church–aisle leads,
        The flag–rope gibbers hoarse,
The home–bound foot–folk wrap their snow–flaked heads,
        Yet I still stalk the course, –
One of us . . . Dark and fair He, dark and fair She, gone:
        The rest—anon.

THE WIND'S PROPHECY

I travel on by barren farms,
And gulls glint out like silver flecks
Against a cloud that speaks of wrecks,
And bellies down with black alarms.
I say: "Thus from my lady's arms
I go; those arms I love the best!"
The wind replies from dip and rise,
"Nay; toward her arms thou journeyest."

Moments of Vision

A distant verge morosely gray
Appears, while clots of flying foam
Break from its muddy monochrome,
And a light blinks up far away.
I sigh: "My eyes now as all day
Behold her ebon loops of hair!"
Like bursting bonds the wind responds,
"Nay, wait for tresses flashing fair!"

From tides the lofty coastlands screen
Come smitings like the slam of doors,
Or hammerings on hollow floors,
As the swell cleaves through caves unseen.
Say I: "Though broad this wild terrene,
Her city home is matched of none!"
From the hoarse skies the wind replies:
"Thou shouldst have said her sea—bord one."

The all—prevailing clouds exclude
The one quick timorous transient star;
The waves outside where breakers are
Huzza like a mad multitude.
"Where the sun ups it, mist—imbued,"
I cry, "there reigns the star for me!"
The wind outshrieks from points and peaks:
"Here, westward, where it downs, mean ye!"

Yonder the headland, vulturine,
Snores like old Skrymer in his sleep,
And every chasm and every steep
Blackens as wakes each pharos—shine.
"I roam, but one is safely mine,"
I say. "God grant she stay my own!"
Low laughs the wind as if it grinned:
"Thy Love is one thou'st not yet known."

Rewritten from an old copy.

DURING WIND AND RAIN

They sing their dearest songs –
He, she, all of them—yea,
Treble and tenor and bass,
    And one to play;
With the candles mooning each face . . .
    Ah, no; the years O!
How the sick leaves reel down in throngs!

They clear the creeping moss –
Elders and juniors—aye,
Making the pathways neat
    And the garden gay;
And they build a shady seat . . .
    Ah, no; the years, the years;
See, the white storm–birds wing across!

They are blithely breakfasting all –
Men and maidens—yea,
Under the summer tree,
    With a glimpse of the bay,
While pet fowl come to the knee . . .
    Ah, no; the years O!
And the rotten rose is ript from the wall.

They change to a high new house,
He, she, all of them—aye,
Clocks and carpets and chairs
    On the lawn all day,
And brightest things that are theirs . . .
    Ah, no; the years, the years;
Down their carved names the rain–drop ploughs.

HE PREFERS HER EARTHLY

This after–sunset is a sight for seeing,
Cliff–heads of craggy cloud surrounding it.
—And dwell you in that glory–show?
You may; for there are strange strange things in being,
    Stranger than I know.

Yet if that chasm of splendour claim your presence
Which glows between the ash cloud and the dun,
    How changed must be your mortal mould!
Changed to a firmament–riding earthless essence
    From what you were of old:

All too unlike the fond and fragile creature
Then known to me . . . Well, shall I say it plain?
    I would not have you thus and there,
But still would grieve on, missing you, still feature
    You as the one you were.

THE DOLLS

"Whenever you dress me dolls, mammy,
    Why do you dress them so,
And make them gallant soldiers,
    When never a one I know;
And not as gentle ladies
    With frills and frocks and curls,
As people dress the dollies
    Of other little girls?"

Ah—why did she not answer:–
    "Because your mammy's heed
Is always gallant soldiers,
    As well may be, indeed.
One of them was your daddy,
    His name I must not tell;
He's not the dad who lives here,
    But one I love too well."

MOLLY GONE

Moments of Vision

No more summer for Molly and me;
     There is snow on the tree,
And the blackbirds plump large as the rooks are, almost,
     And the water is hard
Where they used to dip bills at the dawn ere her figure was lost
     To these coasts, now my prison close—barred.

No more planting by Molly and me
     Where the beds used to be
Of sweet—william; no training the clambering rose
     By the framework of fir
Now bowering the pathway, whereon it swings gaily and blows
     As if calling commendment from her.

No more jauntings by Molly and me
     To the town by the sea,
Or along over Whitesheet to Wynyard's green Gap,
     Catching Montacute Crest
To the right against Sedgmoor, and Corton—Hill's far—distant cap,
     And Pilsdon and Lewsdon to west.

No more singing by Molly to me
     In the evenings when she
Was in mood and in voice, and the candles were lit,
     And past the porch—quoin
The rays would spring out on the laurels; and dumbledores hit
     On the pane, as if wishing to join.

Where, then, is Molly, who's no more with me?
     —As I stand on this lea,
Thinking thus, there's a many—flamed star in the air,
     That tosses a sign
That her glance is regarding its face from her home, so that there
     Her eyes may have meetings with mine.

A BACKWARD SPRING

The trees are afraid to put forth buds,
And there is timidity in the grass;
The plots lie gray where gouged by spuds,
    And whether next week will pass
Free of sly sour winds is the fret of each bush
    Of barberry waiting to bloom.

Yet the snowdrop's face betrays no gloom,
And the primrose pants in its heedless push,
Though the myrtle asks if it's worth the fight
    This year with frost and rime
    To venture one more time
On delicate leaves and buttons of white
From the selfsame bough as at last year's prime,
And never to ruminate on or remember
What happened to it in mid–December.

April 1917.

LOOKING ACROSS

Moments of Vision

I

It is dark in the sky,
And silence is where
Our laughs rang high;
And recall do I
That One is out there.

II

The dawn is not nigh,
And the trees are bare,
And the waterways sigh
That a year has drawn by,
And Two are out there.

III

The wind drops to die
Like the phantom of Care
Too frail for a cry,
And heart brings to eye
That Three are out there.

IV

This Life runs dry
That once ran rare
And rosy in dye,
And fleet the days fly,
And Four are out there.

V

Tired, tired am I
Of this earthly air,
And my wraith asks: Why,
Since these calm lie,
Are not Five out there?

December 1915.

AT A SEASIDE TOWN IN 1869

(Young Lover's Reverie)

I went and stood outside myself,
　　　Spelled the dark sky
　　　And ship–lights nigh,
And grumbling winds that passed thereby.

Then next inside myself I looked,
　　　And there, above
　　　All, shone my Love,
That nothing matched the image of.

Beyond myself again I ranged;
　　　And saw the free
　　　Life by the sea,
And folk indifferent to me.

O 'twas a charm to draw within
　　　Thereafter, where

Moments of Vision

But she was; care
For one thing only, her hid there!

But so it chanced, without myself
    I had to look,
    And then I took
More heed of what I had long forsook:

The boats, the sands, the esplanade,
    The laughing crowd;
    Light—hearted, loud
Greetings from some not ill—endowed;

The evening sunlit cliffs, the talk,
    Hailings and halts,
    The keen sea—salts,
The band, the Morgenblatter Waltz.

Still, when at night I drew inside
    Forward she came,
    Sad, but the same
As when I first had known her name.

Then rose a time when, as by force,
    Outwardly wooed
    By contacts crude,
Her image in abeyance stood . . .

At last I said: This outside life
    Shall not endure;
    I'll seek the pure
Thought—world, and bask in her allure.

Myself again I crept within,
    Scanned with keen care
    The temple where

She'd shone, but could not find her there.

I sought and sought. But O her soul
       Has not since thrown
       Upon my own
One beam! Yea, she is gone, is gone.

From an old note.

THE GLIMPSE

She sped through the door
And, following in haste,
And stirred to the core,
I entered hot–faced;
But I could not find her,
No sign was behind her.
"Where is she?" I said:
– "Who?" they asked that sat there;
"Not a soul's come in sight."
– "A maid with red hair."
– "Ah." They paled. "She is dead.
People see her at night,
But you are the first
On whom she has burst
In the keen common light."

It was ages ago,

When I was quite strong:
I have waited since,—O,
I have waited so long!
– Yea, I set me to own
The house, where now lone
I dwell in void rooms
Booming hollow as tombs!
But I never come near her,
Though nightly I hear her.
And my cheek has grown thin
And my hair has grown gray
With this waiting therein;
But she still keeps away!

THE PEDESTRIAN

AN INCIDENT OF 1883

"Sir, will you let me give you a ride?
Nox Venit, and the heath is wide."
– My phaeton–lantern shone on one
     Young, fair, even fresh,
     But burdened with flesh:
A leathern satchel at his side,
His breathings short, his coat undone.

'Twas as if his corpulent figure slopped
With the shake of his walking when he stopped,
And, though the night's pinch grew acute,

108

Moments of Vision

He wore but a thin
    Wind–thridded suit,
Yet well–shaped shoes for walking in,
Artistic beaver, cane gold–topped.

"Alas, my friend," he said with a smile,
"I am daily bound to foot ten mile –
Wet, dry, or dark—before I rest.
    Six months to live
    My doctors give
Me as my prospect here, at best,
Unless I vamp my sturdiest!"

His voice was that of a man refined,
A man, one well could feel, of mind,
Quite winning in its musical ease;
    But in mould maligned
    By some disease;
And I asked again. But he shook his head;
Then, as if more were due, he said:–

"A student was I—of Schopenhauer,
Kant, Hegel,—and the fountained bower
Of the Muses, too, knew my regard:
    But ah—I fear me
    The grave gapes near me! . . .
Would I could this gross sheath discard,
And rise an ethereal shape, unmarred!"

How I remember him!—his short breath,
His aspect, marked for early death,
As he dropped into the night for ever;
    One caught in his prime
    Of high endeavour;
From all philosophies soon to sever
Through an unconscienced trick of Time!

"WHO'S IN THE NEXT ROOM?"

"Who's in the next room?—who?
  I seemed to see
Somebody in the dawning passing through,
  Unknown to me."
"Nay: you saw nought. He passed invisibly."

"Who's in the next room?—who?
  I seem to hear
Somebody muttering firm in a language new
  That chills the ear."
"No: you catch not his tongue who has entered there."

"Who's in the next room?—who?
  I seem to feel
His breath like a clammy draught, as if it drew
  From the Polar Wheel."
"No: none who breathes at all does the door conceal."

"Who's in the next room?—who?
  A figure wan
With a message to one in there of something due?
  Shall I know him anon?"
"Yea he; and he brought such; and you'll know him anon."

AT A COUNTRY FAIR

At a bygone Western country fair
I saw a giant led by a dwarf
With a red string like a long thin scarf;
How much he was the stronger there
    The giant seemed unaware.

And then I saw that the giant was blind,
And the dwarf a shrewd—eyed little thing;
The giant, mild, timid, obeyed the string
As if he had no independent mind,
    Or will of any kind.

Wherever the dwarf decided to go
At his heels the other trotted meekly,
(Perhaps—I know not—reproaching weakly)
Like one Fate bade that it must be so,
    Whether he wished or no.

Various sights in various climes
I have seen, and more I may see yet,
But that sight never shall I forget,
And have thought it the sorriest of pantomimes,
    If once, a hundred times!

THE MEMORIAL BRASS: 186–

"Why do you weep there, O sweet lady,
    Why do you weep before that brass? –
(I'm a mere student sketching the mediaeval)
    Is some late death lined there, alas? –
Your father's? . . . Well, all pay the debt that paid he!"

"Young man, O must I tell!—My husband's! And under
    His name I set mine, and my DEATH! –
Its date left vacant till my heirs should fill it,
    Stating me faithful till my last breath."
– "Madam, that you are a widow wakes my wonder!"

"O wait! For last month I—remarried!
    And now I fear 'twas a deed amiss.
We've just come home. And I am sick and saddened
    At what the new one will say to this;
And will he think—think that I should have tarried?

"I may add, surely,—with no wish to harm him –
    That he's a temper—yes, I fear!
And when he comes to church next Sunday morning,
    And sees that written . . . O dear, O dear!
– "Madam, I swear your beauty will disarm him!"

HER LOVE-BIRDS

When I looked up at my love-birds
    That Sunday afternoon,
    There was in their tiny tune
A dying fetch like broken words,
When I looked up at my love-birds
    That Sunday afternoon.

When he, too, scanned the love-birds
    On entering there that day,
    'Twas as if he had nought to say
Of his long journey citywards,
When he, too, scanned the love-birds,
    On entering there that day.

And billed and billed the love-birds,
    As 'twere in fond despair
    At the stress of silence where
Had once been tones in tenor thirds,
And billed and billed the love-birds
    As 'twere in fond despair.

O, his speech that chilled the love-birds,
    And smote like death on me,
    As I learnt what was to be,
And knew my life was broke in sherds!
O, his speech that chilled the love-birds,
    And smote like death on me!

PAYING CALLS

I went by footpath and by stile
    Beyond where bustle ends,
Strayed here a mile and there a mile
    And called upon some friends.

On certain ones I had not seen
    For years past did I call,
And then on others who had been
    The oldest friends of all.

It was the time of midsummer
    When they had used to roam;
But now, though tempting was the air,
    I found them all at home.

I spoke to one and other of them
    By mound and stone and tree
Of things we had done ere days were dim,
    But they spoke not to me.

THE UPPER BIRCH–LEAVES

Warm yellowy–green
In the blue serene,
How they skip and sway
On this autumn day!
They cannot know
What has happened below, –
That their boughs down there
Are already quite bare,
That their own will be
When a week has passed, –
For they jig as in glee
To this very last.

But no; there lies
At times in their tune
A note that cries
What at first I fear
I did not hear:
"O we remember
At each wind's hollo –
Though life holds yet –
We go hence soon,
For 'tis November;
– But that you follow
You may forget!"

"IT NEVER LOOKS LIKE SUMMER"

"It never looks like summer here
      On Beeny by the sea."
But though she saw its look as drear,
      Summer it seemed to me.

It never looks like summer now
      Whatever weather's there;
But ah, it cannot anyhow,
      On Beeny or elsewhere!

BOSCASTLE,
March 8, 1913.

EVERYTHING COMES

"The house is bleak and cold
      Built so new for me!
All the winds upon the wold
      Search it through for me;
No screening trees abound,
And the curious eyes around
      Keep on view for me."

"My Love, I am planting trees
      As a screen for you
Both from winds, and eyes that tease

> And peer in for you.
> Only wait till they have grown,
> No such bower will be known
> As I mean for you."

> "Then I will bear it, Love,
> And will wait," she said.
> – So, with years, there grew a grove.
> "Skill how great!" she said.
> "As you wished, Dear?"—"Yes, I see!
> But—I'm dying; and for me
> 'Tis too late," she said.

THE MAN WITH A PAST

> There was merry–making
> When the first dart fell
> As a heralding, –
> Till grinned the fully bared thing,
> And froze like a spell –
> Like a spell.

> Innocent was she,
> Innocent was I,
> Too simple we!
> Before us we did not see,
> Nearing, aught wry –
> Aught wry!

117

I can tell it not now,
It was long ago;
And such things cow;
But that is why and how
Two lives were so –
Were so.

Yes, the years matured,
And the blows were three
That time ensured
On her, which she dumbly endured;
And one on me –
One on me.

HE FEARS HIS GOOD FORTUNE

There was a glorious time
At an epoch of my prime;
Mornings beryl–bespread,
And evenings golden–red;
Nothing gray:
And in my heart I said,
"However this chanced to be,
It is too full for me,
Too rare, too rapturous, rash,
Its spell must close with a crash
Some day!"

The radiance went on
Anon and yet anon,
And sweetness fell around
Like manna on the ground.
　　　"I've no claim,"
Said I, "to be thus crowned:
I am not worthy this:–
Must it not go amiss? –
Well . . . let the end foreseen
Come duly!—I am serene."
—And it came.

HE WONDERS ABOUT HIMSELF

No use hoping, or feeling vext,
Tugged by a force above or under
Like some fantocine, much I wonder
What I shall find me doing next!

Shall I be rushing where bright eyes be?
Shall I be suffering sorrows seven?
Shall I be watching the stars of heaven,
Thinking one of them looks like thee?

Part is mine of the general Will,
Cannot my share in the sum of sources
Bend a digit the poise of forces,

And a fair desire fulfil?

Nov. 1893.

JUBILATE

"The very last time I ever was here," he said,
"I saw much less of the quick than I saw of the dead."
– He was a man I had met with somewhere before,
But how or when I now could recall no more.

"The hazy mazy moonlight at one in the morning
Spread out as a sea across the frozen snow,
Glazed to live sparkles like the great breastplate adorning
The priest of the Temple, with Urim and Thummim aglow.

"The yew–tree arms, glued hard to the stiff stark air,
Hung still in the village sky as theatre–scenes
When I came by the churchyard wall, and halted there
At a shut–in sound of fiddles and tambourines.

"And as I stood hearkening, dulcimers, haut–boys, and shawms,
And violoncellos, and a three–stringed double–bass,
Joined in, and were intermixed with a singing of psalms;
And I looked over at the dead men's dwelling–place.

"Through the shine of the slippery snow I now could see,
As it were through a crystal roof, a great company

Of the dead minueting in stately step underground
To the tune of the instruments I had before heard sound.

"It was 'Eden New,' and dancing they sang in a chore,
'We are out of it all!—yea, in Little–Ease cramped no more!'
And their shrouded figures pacing with joy I could see
As you see the stage from the gallery. And they had no heed of me.

"And I lifted my head quite dazed from the churchyard wall
And I doubted not that it warned I should soon have my call.
But—" . . . Then in the ashes he emptied the dregs of his cup,
And onward he went, and the darkness swallowed him up.

HE REVISITS HIS FIRST SCHOOL

I should not have shown in the flesh,
I ought to have gone as a ghost;
It was awkward, unseemly almost,
Standing solidly there as when fresh,
        Pink, tiny, crisp–curled,
        My pinions yet furled
        From the winds of the world.

After waiting so many a year
To wait longer, and go as a sprite
From the tomb at the mid of some night
Was the right, radiant way to appear;
        Not as one wanzing weak

From life's roar and reek,
His rest still to seek:

Yea, beglimpsed through the quaint quarried glass
Of green moonlight, by me greener made,
When they'd cry, perhaps, "There sits his shade
In his olden haunt—just as he was
  When in Walkingame he
  Conned the grand Rule–of–Three
  With the bent of a bee."

But to show in the afternoon sun,
With an aspect of hollow–eyed care,
When none wished to see me come there,
Was a garish thing, better undone.
  Yes; wrong was the way;
  But yet, let me say,
  I may right it—some day.

"I THOUGHT, MY HEART"

I thought, my Heart, that you had healed
Of those sore smartings of the past,
And that the summers had oversealed
  All mark of them at last.
But closely scanning in the night
I saw them standing crimson–bright
   Just as she made them:

Nothing could fade them;
Yea, I can swear
That there they were –
They still were there!

Then the Vision of her who cut them came,
And looking over my shoulder said,
"I am sure you deal me all the blame
        For those sharp smarts and red;
But meet me, dearest, to–morrow night,
In the churchyard at the moon's half–height,
            And so strange a kiss
            Shall be mine, I wis,
            That you'll cease to know
            If the wounds you show
            Be there or no!"

FRAGMENT

At last I entered a long dark gallery,
        Catacomb–lined; and ranged at the side
        Were the bodies of men from far and wide
Who, motion past, were nevertheless not dead.

"The sense of waiting here strikes strong;
        Everyone's waiting, waiting, it seems to me;
        What are you waiting for so long? –
What is to happen?" I said.

"O we are waiting for one called God," said they,
  "(Though by some the Will, or Force, or Laws;
  And, vaguely, by some, the Ultimate Cause;)
Waiting for him to see us before we are clay.
Yes; waiting, waiting, for God TO KNOW IT" . . .

  "To know what?" questioned I.
"To know how things have been going on earth and below it:
  It is clear he must know some day."
  I thereon asked them why.

"Since he made us humble pioneers
Of himself in consciousness of Life's tears,
It needs no mighty prophecy
To tell that what he could mindlessly show
His creatures, he himself will know.

"By some still close—cowled mystery
We have reached feeling faster than he,
But he will overtake us anon,
  If the world goes on."

MIDNIGHT ON THE GREAT WESTERN

In the third—class seat sat the journeying boy,
  And the roof—lamp's oily flame
Played down on his listless form and face,

Bewrapt past knowing to what he was going,
        Or whence he came.

In the band of his hat the journeying boy
        Had a ticket stuck; and a string
Around his neck bore the key of his box,
That twinkled gleams of the lamp's sad beams
        Like a living thing.

What past can be yours, O journeying boy
        Towards a world unknown,
Who calmly, as if incurious quite
On all at stake, can undertake
        This plunge alone?

Knows your soul a sphere, O journeying boy,
        Our rude realms far above,
Whence with spacious vision you mark and mete
This region of sin that you find you in,
        But are not of?

HONEYMOON TIME AT AN INN

At the shiver of morning, a little before the false dawn,
        The moon was at the window—square,
        Deedily brooding in deformed decay —
        The curve hewn off her cheek as by an adze;
At the shiver of morning a little before the false dawn

Moments of Vision

So the moon looked in there.

Her speechless eyeing reached across the chamber,
       Where lay two souls opprest,
    One a white lady sighing, "Why am I sad!"
    To him who sighed back, "Sad, my Love, am I!"
And speechlessly the old moon conned the chamber,
       And these two reft of rest.

While their large–pupilled vision swept the scene there,
       Nought seeming imminent,
    Something fell sheer, and crashed, and from the floor
    Lay glittering at the pair with a shattered gaze,
While their large–pupilled vision swept the scene there,
       And the many–eyed thing outleant.

With a start they saw that it was an old–time pier–glass
       Which had stood on the mantel near,
    Its silvering blemished,—yes, as if worn away
    By the eyes of the countless dead who had smirked at it
Ere these two ever knew that old–time pier–glass
       And its vague and vacant leer.

As he looked, his bride like a moth skimmed forth, and kneeling
       Quick, with quivering sighs,
    Gathered the pieces under the moon's sly ray,
    Unwitting as an automaton what she did;
Till he entreated, hasting to where she was kneeling,
       Let it stay where it lies!"

"Long years of sorrow this means!" breathed the lady
       As they retired. "Alas!"
    And she lifted one pale hand across her eyes.
    "Don't trouble, Love; it's nothing," the bridegroom said.
"Long years of sorrow for us!" murmured the lady,
       "Or ever this evil pass!"

And the Spirits Ironic laughed behind the wainscot,
   And the Spirits of Pity sighed.
  It's good," said the Spirits Ironic, "to tickle their minds
  With a portent of their wedlock's after–grinds."
And the Spirits of Pity sighed behind the wainscot,
  "It's a portent we cannot abide!

"More, what shall happen to prove the truth of the portent?"
   —"Oh; in brief, they will fade till old,
  And their loves grow numbed ere death, by the cark of care."
– "But nought see we that asks for portents there? –
'Tis the lot of all."—"Well, no less true is a portent
  That it fits all mortal mould."

THE ROBIN

When up aloft
I fly and fly,
I see in pools
The shining sky,
And a happy bird
Am I, am I!

When I descend
Towards their brink
I stand, and look,
And stoop, and drink,

127

And bathe my wings,
And chink and prink.

When winter frost
Makes earth as steel
I search and search
But find no meal,
And most unhappy
Then I feel.

But when it lasts,
And snows still fall,
I get to feel
No grief at all,
For I turn to a cold stiff
Feathery ball!

"I ROSE AND WENT TO ROU'TOR TOWN"

(She, alone)

I rose and went to Rou'tor Town
  With gaiety and good heart,
  And ardour for the start,
That morning ere the moon was down
That lit me off to Rou'tor Town
  With gaiety and good heart.

When sojourn soon at Rou'tor Town

Wrote sorrows on my face,
I strove that none should trace
The pale and gray, once pink and brown,
When sojourn soon at Rou'tor Town
Wrote sorrows on my face.

The evil wrought at Rou'tor Town
On him I'd loved so true
I cannot tell anew:
But nought can quench, but nought can drown
The evil wrought at Rou'tor Town
On him I'd loved so true!

THE NETTLES

This, then, is the grave of my son,
Whose heart she won! And nettles grow
Upon his mound; and she lives just below.

How he upbraided me, and left,
And our lives were cleft, because I said
She was hard, unfeeling, caring but to wed.

Well, to see this sight I have fared these miles,
And her firelight smiles from her window there,
Whom he left his mother to cherish with tender care!

It is enough. I'll turn and go;

Yes, nettles grow where lone lies he,
Who spurned me for seeing what he could not see.

IN A WAITING-ROOM

On a morning sick as the day of doom
     With the drizzling gray
     Of an English May,
There were few in the railway waiting-room.
About its walls were framed and varnished
Pictures of liners, fly-blown, tarnished.
The table bore a Testament
For travellers' reading, if suchwise bent.

     I read it on and on,
     And, thronging the Gospel of Saint John,
     Were figures—additions, multiplications –
By some one scrawled, with sundry emendations;
     Not scoffingly designed,
     But with an absent mind, –
Plainly a bagman's counts of cost,
What he had profited, what lost;
And whilst I wondered if there could have been
     Any particle of a soul
     In that poor man at all,

     To cypher rates of wage
     Upon that printed page,

There joined in the charmless scene
And stood over me and the scribbled book
    (To lend the hour's mean hue
    A smear of tragedy too)
A soldier and wife, with haggard look
Subdued to stone by strong endeavour;
    And then I heard
    From a casual word
They were parting as they believed for ever.

    But next there came
    Like the eastern flame
Of some high altar, children—a pair –
Who laughed at the fly–blown pictures there.
"Here are the lovely ships that we,
Mother, are by and by going to see!
When we get there it's 'most sure to be fine,
And the band will play, and the sun will shine!"

It rained on the skylight with a din
As we waited and still no train came in;
But the words of the child in the squalid room
Had spread a glory through the gloom.

THE CLOCK–WINDER

It is dark as a cave,
Or a vault in the nave

Moments of Vision

When the iron door
Is closed, and the floor
Of the church relaid
With trowel and spade.

But the parish–clerk
Cares not for the dark
As he winds in the tower
At a regular hour
The rheumatic clock,
Whose dilatory knock
You can hear when praying
At the day's decaying,
Or at any lone while
From a pew in the aisle.

Up, up from the ground
Around and around
In the turret stair
He clambers, to where
The wheelwork is,
With its tick, click, whizz,
Reposefully measuring
Each day to its end
That mortal men spend
In sorrowing and pleasuring
Nightly thus does he climb
To the trackway of Time.

Him I followed one night
To this place without light,
And, ere I spoke, heard
Him say, word by word,
At the end of his winding,
The darkness unminding:–

"So I wipe out one more,
My Dear, of the sore
Sad days that still be,
Like a drying Dead Sea,
Between you and me!"

Who she was no man knew:
He had long borne him blind
To all womankind;
And was ever one who
Kept his past out of view.

OLD EXCURSIONS

"What's the good of going to Ridgeway,
        Cerne, or Sydling Mill,
        Or to Yell'ham Hill,
Blithely bearing Casterbridge—way
        As we used to do?
She will no more climb up there,
Or be visible anywhere
        In those haunts we knew."

But to—night, while walking weary,
        Near me seemed her shade,
        Come as 'twere to upbraid
This my mood in deeming dreary
        Scenes that used to please;

And, if she did come to me,
Still solicitous, there may be
     Good in going to these.

So, I'll care to roam to Ridgeway,
     Cerne, or Sydling Mill,
     Or to Yell'ham Hill,
Blithely bearing Casterbridge–way
     As we used to do,
Since her phasm may flit out there,
And may greet me anywhere
     In those haunts we knew.

April 1913.

THE MASKED FACE

I found me in a great surging space,
     At either end a door,
And I said: "What is this giddying place,
     With no firm–fixed floor,
     That I knew not of before?"
     "It is Life," said a mask–clad face.

I asked: "But how do I come here,
     Who never wished to come;
Can the light and air be made more clear,
     The floor more quietsome,

And the doors set wide? They numb
Fast—locked, and fill with fear."

The mask put on a bleak smile then,
    And said, "O vassal—wight,
There once complained a goosequill pen
    To the scribe of the Infinite
    Of the words it had to write
Because they were past its ken."

IN A WHISPERING GALLERY

That whisper takes the voice
Of a Spirit's compassionings
Close, but invisible,
And throws me under a spell
At the kindling vision it brings,
And for a moment I rejoice,
And believe in transcendent things
That would mould from this muddy earth
A spot for the splendid birth
Of everlasting lives,
Whereto no night arrives;
And this gaunt gray gallery
A tabernacle of worth
On this drab—aired afternoon,
When you can barely see
Across its hazed lacune

If opposite aught there be
Of fleshed humanity
Wherewith I may commune;
Or if the voice so near
Be a soul's voice floating here.

THE SOMETHING THAT SAVED HIM

It was when
Whirls of thick waters laved me
Again and again,
That something arose and saved me;
Yea, it was then.

In that day
Unseeing the azure went I
On my way,
And to white winter bent I,
Knowing no May.

Reft of renown,
Under the night clouds beating
Up and down,
In my needfulness greeting
Cit and clown.

Long there had been
Much of a murky colour

In the scene,
Dull prospects meeting duller;
    Nought between.

    Last, there loomed
A closing–in blind alley,
    Though there boomed
A feeble summons to rally
    Where it gloomed.

    The clock rang;
The hour brought a hand to deliver;
    I upsprang,
And looked back at den, ditch and river,
    And sang.

THE ENEMY'S PORTRAIT

He saw the portrait of his enemy, offered
At auction in a street he journeyed nigh,
That enemy, now late dead, who in his life–time
Had injured deeply him the passer–by.
"To get that picture, pleased be God, I'll try,
And utterly destroy it; and no more
Shall be inflicted on man's mortal eye
A countenance so sinister and sore!"

And so he bought the painting. Driving homeward,

Moments of Vision

"The frame will come in useful," he declared,
"The rest is fuel." On his arrival, weary,
Asked what he bore with him, and how he fared,
He said he had bid for a picture, though he cared
For the frame only: on the morrow he
Would burn the canvas, which could well be spared,
Seeing that it portrayed his enemy.

Next day some other duty found him busy;
The foe was laid his face against the wall;
But on the next he set himself to loosen
The straining–strips. And then a casual call
Prevented his proceeding therewithal;
And thus the picture waited, day by day,
Its owner's pleasure, like a wretched thrall,
Until a month and more had slipped away.

And then upon a morn he found it shifted,
Hung in a corner by a servitor.
"Why did you take on you to hang that picture?
You know it was the frame I bought it for."
"It stood in the way of every visitor,
And I just hitched it there."—"Well, it must go:
I don't commemorate men whom I abhor.
Remind me 'tis to do. The frame I'll stow."

But things become forgotten. In the shadow
Of the dark corner hung it by its string,
And there it stayed—once noticed by its owner,
Who said, "Ah me—I must destroy that thing!"
But when he died, there, none remembering,
It hung, till moved to prominence, as one sees;
And comers pause and say, examining,
"I thought they were the bitterest enemies?"

IMAGININGS

She saw herself a lady
    With fifty frocks in wear,
And rolling wheels, and rooms the best,
    And faithful maidens' care,
And open lawns and shady
    For weathers warm or drear.

She found herself a striver,
    All liberal gifts debarred,
With days of gloom, and movements stressed,
    And early visions marred,
And got no man to wive her
    But one whose lot was hard.

Yet in the moony night-time
    She steals to stile and lea
During his heavy slumberous rest
    When homecome wearily,
And dreams of some blest bright-time
    She knows can never be.

ON THE DOORSTEP

The rain imprinted the step's wet shine
With target–circles that quivered and crossed
As I was leaving this porch of mine;
When from within there swelled and paused
      A song's sweet note;
   And back I turned, and thought,
      "Here I'll abide."

The step shines wet beneath the rain,
Which prints its circles as heretofore;
I watch them from the porch again,
But no song–notes within the door
      Now call to me
   To shun the dripping lea
      And forth I stride.

Jan. 1914.

SIGNS AND TOKENS

Said the red–cloaked crone
In a whispered moan:

Moments of Vision

"The dead man was limp
When laid in his chest;
Yea, limp; and why
But to signify
That the grave will crimp
Ere next year's sun
Yet another one
Of those in that house –
It may be the best –
For its endless drowse!"

Said the brown–shawled dame
To confirm the same:

"And the slothful flies
On the rotting fruit
Have been seen to wear
While crawling there
Crape scarves, by eyes
That were quick and acute;
As did those that had pitched
On the cows by the pails,
And with flaps of their tails
Were far away switched."

Said the third in plaid,
Each word being weighed:

"And trotting does
In the park, in the lane,
And just outside
The shuttered pane,
Have also been heard –
Quick feet as light
As the feet of a sprite –

And the wise mind knows
What things may betide
When such has occurred."

Cried the black—craped fourth,
Cold faced as the north:

"O, though giving such
Some head—room, I smile
At your falterings
When noting those things
Round your domicile!
For what, what can touch
One whom, riven of all
That makes life gay,
No hints can appal
Of more takings away!"

PATHS OF FORMER TIME

No; no;
It must not be so:
They are the ways we do not go.

Still chew
The kine, and moo
In the meadows we used to wander through;

Still purl
The rivulets and curl
Towards the weirs with a musical swirl;

Haymakers
As in former years
Rake rolls into heaps that the pitchfork rears;

Wheels crack
On the turfy track
The waggon pursues with its toppling pack.

"Why then shun –
Since summer's not done –
All this because of the lack of one?"

Had you been
Sharer of that scene
You would not ask while it bites in keen

Why it is so
We can no more go
By the summer paths we used to know!

1913.

THE CLOCK OF THE YEARS

Moments of Vision

"A spirit passed before my face; the hair of my flesh stood up."

And the Spirit said,
"I can make the clock of the years go backward,
But am loth to stop it where you will."
  And I cried, "Agreed
  To that. Proceed:
  It's better than dead!"

He answered, "Peace";
And called her up—as last before me;
Then younger, younger she freshed, to the year
  I first had known
  Her woman–grown,
  And I cried, "Cease! –

"Thus far is good –
It is enough—let her stay thus always!"
But alas for me. He shook his head:
  No stop was there;
  And she waned child–fair,
  And to babyhood.

Still less in mien
To my great sorrow became she slowly,
And smalled till she was nought at all
  In his checkless griff;
  And it was as if
  She had never been.

"Better," I plained,
"She were dead as before! The memory of her
Had lived in me; but it cannot now!"
  And coldly his voice:
  "It was your choice
  To mar the ordained."

1916.

AT THE PIANO

A woman was playing,
    A man looking on;
    And the mould of her face,
    And her neck, and her hair,
    Which the rays fell upon
    Of the two candles there,
Sent him mentally straying
    In some fancy-place
    Where pain had no trace.

A cowled Apparition
    Came pushing between;
    And her notes seemed to sigh,
    And the lights to burn pale,
    As a spell numbed the scene.
    But the maid saw no bale,
And the man no monition;
    And Time laughed awry,
    And the Phantom hid nigh.

THE SHADOW ON THE STONE

I went by the Druid stone
That broods in the garden white and lone,
And I stopped and looked at the shifting shadows
That at some moments fall thereon
From the tree hard by with a rhythmic swing,
And they shaped in my imagining
To the shade that a well–known head and shoulders
Threw there when she was gardening.

I thought her behind my back,
Yea, her I long had learned to lack,
And I said: "I am sure you are standing behind me,
Though how do you get into this old track?"
And there was no sound but the fall of a leaf
As a sad response; and to keep down grief
I would not turn my head to discover
That there was nothing in my belief.

Yet I wanted to look and see
That nobody stood at the back of me;
But I thought once more: "Nay, I'll not unvision
A shape which, somehow, there may be."
So I went on softly from the glade,
And left her behind me throwing her shade,
As she were indeed an apparition –
My head unturned lest my dream should fade.

Begun 1913: finished 1916.

146

IN THE GARDEN

(M. H.)

We waited for the sun
To break its cloudy prison
(For day was not yet done,
And night still unbegun)
Leaning by the dial.

After many a trial –
We all silent there –
It burst as new–arisen,
Throwing a shade to where
Time travelled at that minute.

Little saw we in it,
But this much I know,
Of lookers on that shade,
Her towards whom it made
Soonest had to go.

1915.

THE TREE AND THE LADY

      I have done all I could
For that lady I knew! Through the heats I have shaded her,
Drawn to her songsters when summer has jaded her,
      Home from the heath or the wood.

      At the mirth–time of May,
When my shadow first lured her, I'd donned my new bravery
Of greenth: 'twas my all. Now I shiver in slavery,
      Icicles grieving me gray.

      Plumed to every twig's end
I could tempt her chair under me. Much did I treasure her
During those days she had nothing to pleasure her;
      Mutely she used me as friend.

      I'm a skeleton now,
And she's gone, craving warmth. The rime sticks like a skin to me;
Through me Arcturus peers; Nor'lights shoot into me;
      Gone is she, scorning my bough!

AN UPBRAIDING

Now I am dead you sing to me
      The songs we used to know,
But while I lived you had no wish
      Or care for doing so.

Now I am dead you come to me
      In the moonlight, comfortless;
Ah, what would I have given alive
      To win such tenderness!

When you are dead, and stand to me
      Not differenced, as now,
But like again, will you be cold
      As when we lived, or how?

THE YOUNG GLASS–STAINER

"These Gothic windows, how they wear me out
With cusp and foil, and nothing straight or square,
Crude colours, leaden borders roundabout,
And fitting in Peter here, and Matthew there!

"What a vocation! Here do I draw now
The abnormal, loving the Hellenic norm;
Martha I paint, and dream of Hera's brow,
Mary, and think of Aphrodite's form."

Nov. 1893.

LOOKING AT A PICTURE ON AN ANNIVERSARY

But don't you know it, my dear,
    Don't you know it,
That this day of the year
(What rainbow–rays embow it!)
We met, strangers confessed,
    But parted—blest?

Though at this query, my dear,
    There in your frame
Unmoved you still appear,
You must be thinking the same,
But keep that look demure
    Just to allure.

And now at length a trace
    I surely vision
Upon that wistful face
Of old–time recognition,
Smiling forth, "Yes, as you say,
    It is the day."

For this one phase of you
    Now left on earth
This great date must endue
With pulsings of rebirth? –
I see them vitalize

    Those two deep eyes!

But if this face I con
        Does not declare
Consciousness living on
Still in it, little I care
To live myself, my dear,
        Lone–labouring here!

Spring 1913.

THE CHOIRMASTER'S BURIAL

He often would ask us
That, when he died,
After playing so many
To their last rest,
If out of us any
Should here abide,
And it would not task us,
We would with our lutes
Play over him
By his grave–brim
The psalm he liked best –
The one whose sense suits
"Mount Ephraim" –
And perhaps we should seem
To him, in Death's dream,

Moments of Vision

Like the seraphim.

As soon as I knew
That his spirit was gone
I thought this his due,
And spoke thereupon.
"I think," said the vicar,
"A read service quicker
Than viols out–of–doors
In these frosts and hoars.
That old–fashioned way
Requires a fine day,
And it seems to me
It had better not be."

Hence, that afternoon,
Though never knew he
That his wish could not be,
To get through it faster
They buried the master
Without any tune.

But 'twas said that, when
At the dead of next night
The vicar looked out,
There struck on his ken
Thronged roundabout,
Where the frost was graying
The headstoned grass,
A band all in white
Like the saints in church–glass,
Singing and playing
The ancient stave
By the choirmaster's grave.

Such the tenor man told

When he had grown old.

THE MAN WHO FORGOT

At a lonely cross where bye—roads met
    I sat upon a gate;
I saw the sun decline and set,
    And still was fain to wait.

A trotting boy passed up the way
    And roused me from my thought;
I called to him, and showed where lay
    A spot I shyly sought.

"A summer—house fair stands hidden where
    You see the moonlight thrown;
Go, tell me if within it there
    A lady sits alone."

He half demurred, but took the track,
    And silence held the scene;
I saw his figure rambling back;
    I asked him if he had been.

"I went just where you said, but found
    No summer—house was there:
Beyond the slope 'tis all bare ground;
    Nothing stands anywhere.

"A man asked what my brains were worth;
    The house, he said, grew rotten,
And was pulled down before my birth,
    And is almost forgotten!"

My right mind woke, and I stood dumb;
    Forty years' frost and flower
Had fleeted since I'd used to come
    To meet her in that bower.

WHILE DRAWING IN A CHURCH–YARD

"It is sad that so many of worth,
    Still in the flesh," soughed the yew,
"Misjudge their lot whom kindly earth
    Secludes from view.

"They ride their diurnal round
    Each day–span's sum of hours
In peerless ease, without jolt or bound
    Or ache like ours.

"If the living could but hear
    What is heard by my roots as they creep
Round the restful flock, and the things said there,
    No one would weep."

154

"'Now set among the wise,'
They say: 'Enlarged in scope,
That no God trumpet us to rise
        We truly hope.'"

I listened to his strange tale
    In the mood that stillness brings,
And I grew to accept as the day wore pale
    That show of things.

"FOR LIFE I HAD NEVER CARED GREATLY"

For Life I had never cared greatly,
        As worth a man's while;
        Peradventures unsought,
    Peradventures that finished in nought,
Had kept me from youth and through manhood till lately
        Unwon by its style.

In earliest years—why I know not –
        I viewed it askance;
        Conditions of doubt,
    Conditions that leaked slowly out,
May haply have bent me to stand and to show not
        Much zest for its dance.

With symphonies soft and sweet colour
        It courted me then,

155

Till evasions seemed wrong,
Till evasions gave in to its song,
And I warmed, until living aloofly loomed duller
Than life among men.

Anew I found nought to set eyes on,
When, lifting its hand,
It uncloaked a star,
Uncloaked it from fog–damps afar,
And showed its beams burning from pole to horizon
As bright as a brand.

And so, the rough highway forgetting,
I pace hill and dale
Regarding the sky,
Regarding the vision on high,
And thus re–illumed have no humour for letting
My pilgrimage fail.

POEMS OF WAR AND PATRIOTISM:

"MEN WHO MARCH AWAY"

(SONG OF THE SOLDIERS)

What of the faith and fire within us
Men who march away
Ere the barn–cocks say

Moments of Vision

Night is growing gray,
Leaving all that here can win us;
What of the faith and fire within us
    Men who march away?

Is it a purblind prank, O think you,
    Friend with the musing eye,
    Who watch us stepping by
    With doubt and dolorous sigh?
Can much pondering so hoodwink you!
Is it a purblind prank, O think you,
    Friend with the musing eye?

Nay. We well see what we are doing,
    Though some may not see –
    Dalliers as they be –
    England's need are we;
Her distress would leave us rueing:
Nay. We well see what we are doing,
    Though some may not see!

In our heart of hearts believing
    Victory crowns the just,
    And that braggarts must
    Surely bite the dust,
Press we to the field ungrieving,
In our heart of hearts believing
    Victory crowns the just.

Hence the faith and fire within us
    Men who march away
    Ere the barn–cocks say
    Night is growing gray,
Leaving all that here can win us;
Hence the faith and fire within us
    Men who march away.

September 5, 1914.

HIS COUNTRY

[He travels southward, and looks around;]
I journeyed from my native spot
  Across the south sea shine,
And found that people in hall and cot
Laboured and suffered each his lot
  Even as I did mine.

[and cannot discern the boundary]
Thus noting them in meads and marts
  It did not seem to me
That my dear country with its hearts,
Minds, yearnings, worse and better parts
  Had ended with the sea.

[of his native country;]
I further and further went anon,
  As such I still surveyed,
And further yet—yea, on and on,
And all the men I looked upon
  Had heart–strings fellow–made.

[or where his duties to his fellow–creatures end;]
I traced the whole terrestrial round,

Homing the other side;
Then said I, "What is there to bound
My denizenship? It seems I have found
    Its scope to be world–wide."

[nor who are his enemies]
I asked me: "Whom have I to fight,
    And whom have I to dare,
And whom to weaken, crush, and blight?
My country seems to have kept in sight
    On my way everywhere."

1913.

ENGLAND TO GERMANY IN 1914

"O England, may God punish thee!"
– Is it that Teuton genius flowers
Only to breathe malignity
Upon its friend of earlier hours?
– We have eaten your bread, you have eaten ours,
We have loved your burgs, your pines' green moan,
Fair Rhine–stream, and its storied towers;
Your shining souls of deathless dowers
Have won us as they were our own:

We have nursed no dreams to shed your blood,
We have matched your might not rancorously,

Save a flushed few whose blatant mood
You heard and marked as well as we
To tongue not in their country's key;
But yet you cry with face aflame,
"O England, may God punish thee!"
And foul in onward history,
And present sight, your ancient name.

Autumn 1914.

ON THE BELGIAN EXPATRIATION

I dreamt that people from the Land of Chimes
Arrived one autumn morning with their bells,
To hoist them on the towers and citadels
Of my own country, that the musical rhymes

Rung by them into space at meted times
Amid the market's daily stir and stress,
And the night's empty star—lit silentness,
Might solace souls of this and kindred climes.

Then I awoke; and lo, before me stood
The visioned ones, but pale and full of fear;
From Bruges they came, and Antwerp, and Ostend,

No carillons in their train. Foes of mad mood
Had shattered these to shards amid the gear

Of ravaged roof, and smouldering gable–end.

October 18, 1914.

AN APPEAL TO AMERICA ON BEHALF OF THE BELGIAN DESTITUTE

Seven millions stand
Emaciate, in that ancient Delta land:
We here, full–charged with our own maimed and dead,
And coiled in throbbing conflicts slow and sore,
Can poorly soothe these ails unmerited
Of souls forlorn upon the facing shore! –
Where naked, gaunt, in endless band on band
Seven millions stand.

No man can say
To your great country that, with scant delay,
You must, perforce, ease them in their loud need:
We know that nearer first your duty lies;
But—is it much to ask that you let plead
Your lovingkindness with you—wooing–wise –
Albeit that aught you owe, and must repay,
No man can say?

December 1914.

THE PITY OF IT

I walked in loamy Wessex lanes, afar
From rail–track and from highway, and I heard
In field and farmstead many an ancient word
Of local lineage like "Thu bist," "Er war,"

"Ich woll," "Er sholl," and by–talk similar,
Nigh as they speak who in this month's moon gird
At England's very loins, thereunto spurred
By gangs whose glory threats and slaughters are.

Then seemed a Heart crying: "Whosoever they be
At root and bottom of this, who flung this flame
Between kin folk kin tongued even as are we,

"Sinister, ugly, lurid, be their fame;
May their familiars grow to shun their name,
And their brood perish everlastingly."

April 1915.

IN TIME OF WARS AND TUMULTS

"Would that I'd not drawn breath here!" some one said,
"To stalk upon this stage of evil deeds,
Where purposelessly month by month proceeds
A play so sorely shaped and blood–bespread."

Yet had his spark not quickened, but lain dead
To the gross spectacles of this our day,
And never put on the proffered cloak of clay,
He had but known not things now manifested;

Life would have swirled the same. Morns would have dawned
On the uprooting by the night–gun's stroke
Of what the yester noonshine brought to flower;

Brown martial brows in dying throes have wanned
Despite his absence; hearts no fewer been broke
By Empery's insatiate lust of power.

1915.

IN TIME OF "THE BREAKING OF NATIONS" {1}

I

Only a man harrowing clods
   In a slow silent walk

With an old horse that stumbles and nods
    Half asleep as they stalk.

II

Only thin smoke without flame
    From the heaps of couch–grass;
Yet this will go onward the same
    Though Dynasties pass.

III

Yonder a maid and her wight
    Come whispering by:
War's annals will cloud into night
    Ere their story die.

1915.

CRY OF THE HOMELESS

AFTER THE PRUSSIAN INVASION OF BELGIUM

"Instigator of the ruin –
    Whichsoever thou mayst be
Of the masterful of Europe
    That contrived our misery –
Hear the wormwood–worded greeting
    From each city, shore, and lea

>   Of thy victims:
>   "Conqueror, all hail to thee!"
>
> "Yea: 'All hail!' we grimly shout thee
>   That wast author, fount, and head
> Of these wounds, whoever proven
>   When our times are throughly read.
> 'May thy loved be slighted, blighted,
>   And forsaken,' be it said
>   By thy victims,
>   'And thy children beg their bread!'
>
> "Nay: a richer malediction! –
>   Rather let this thing befall
> In time's hurling and unfurling
>   On the night when comes thy call;
> That compassion dew thy pillow
>   And bedrench thy senses all
>   For thy victims,
>   Till death dark thee with his pall."

August 1915.

BEFORE MARCHING AND AFTER

(in Memoriam F. W. G.)

>   Orion swung southward aslant
>   Where the starved Egdon pine-trees had thinned,

Moments of Vision

The Pleiads aloft seemed to pant
With the heather that twitched in the wind;
But he looked on indifferent to sights such as these,
Unswayed by love, friendship, home joy or home sorrow,
And wondered to what he would march on the morrow.

The crazed household–clock with its whirr
Rang midnight within as he stood,
He heard the low sighing of her
Who had striven from his birth for his good;
But he still only asked the spring starlight, the breeze,
What great thing or small thing his history would borrow
From that Game with Death he would play on the morrow.

When the heath wore the robe of late summer,
And the fuchsia–bells, hot in the sun,
Hung red by the door, a quick comer
Brought tidings that marching was done
For him who had joined in that game overseas
Where Death stood to win, though his name was to borrow
A brightness therefrom not to fade on the morrow.

September 1915.

"OFTEN WHEN WARRING"

Often when warring for he wist not what,
An enemy–soldier, passing by one weak,

Has tendered water, wiped the burning cheek,
And cooled the lips so black and clammed and hot;

Then gone his way, and maybe quite forgot
The deed of grace amid the roar and reck;
Yet larger vision than loud arms bespeak
He there has reached, although he has known it not.

For natural mindsight, triumphing in the act
Over the throes of artificial rage,
Has thuswise muffled victory's peal of pride,
Rended to ribands policy's specious page
That deals but with evasion, code, and pact,
And war's apology wholly stultified.

1915.

THEN AND NOW

When battles were fought
With a chivalrous sense of Should and Ought,
In spirit men said,
"End we quick or dead,
Honour is some reward!
Let us fight fair—for our own best or worst;
So, Gentlemen of the Guard,
Fire first!"

In the open they stood,
Man to man in his knightlihood:
     They would not deign
     To profit by a stain
     On the honourable rules,
Knowing that practise perfidy no man durst
     Who in the heroic schools
          Was nurst.

     But now, behold, what
Is warfare wherein honour is not!
     Rama laments
     Its dead innocents:
     Herod breathes: "Sly slaughter
Shall rule! Let us, by modes once called accurst,
     Overhead, under water,
          Stab first."

1915.

A CALL TO NATIONAL SERVICE

Up and be doing, all who have a hand
To lift, a back to bend. It must not be
In times like these that vaguely linger we
To air our vaunts and hopes; and leave our land

Untended as a wild of weeds and sand.

– Say, then, "I come!" and go, O women and men
Of palace, ploughshare, easel, counter, pen;
That scareless, scathless, England still may stand.

Would years but let me stir as once I stirred
At many a dawn to take the forward track,
And with a stride plunged on to enterprize,

I now would speed like yester wind that whirred
Through yielding pines; and serve with never a slack,
So loud for promptness all around outcries!

March 1917.

THE DEAD AND THE LIVING ONE

The dead woman lay in her first night's grave,
And twilight fell from the clouds' concave,
And those she had asked to forgive forgave.

The woman passing came to a pause
By the heaped white shapes of wreath and cross,
And looked upon where the other was.

And as she mused there thus spoke she:
"Never your countenance did I see,
But you've been a good good friend to me!"

Moments of Vision

Rose a plaintive voice from the sod below:
"O woman whose accents I do not know,
What is it that makes you approve me so?"

"O dead one, ere my soldier went,
I heard him saying, with warm intent,
To his friend, when won by your blandishment:

"'I would change for that lass here and now!
And if I return I may break my vow
To my present Love, and contrive somehow

"'To call my own this new–found pearl,
Whose eyes have the light, whose lips the curl,
I always have looked for in a girl!'

"—And this is why that by ceasing to be –
Though never your countenance did I see –
You prove you a good good friend to me;

"And I pray each hour for your soul's repose
In gratitude for your joining those
No lover will clasp when his campaigns close."

Away she turned, when arose to her eye
A martial phantom of gory dye,
That said, with a thin and far–off sigh:

"O sweetheart, neither shall I clasp you,
For the foe this day has pierced me through,
And sent me to where she is. Adieu! –

"And forget not when the night–wind's whine
Calls over this turf where her limbs recline,
That it travels on to lament by mine."

There was a cry by the white–flowered mound,
There was a laugh from underground,
There was a deeper gloom around.

1915.

A NEW YEAR'S EVE IN WAR TIME

I

      Phantasmal fears,
      And the flap of the flame,
      And the throb of the clock,
      And a loosened slate,
      And the blind night's drone,
Which tiredly the spectral pines intone!

II

And the blood in my ears
Strumming always the same,
And the gable–cock
With its fitful grate,
And myself, alone.

III

The twelfth hour nears

171

Hand–hid, as in shame;
I undo the lock,
And listen, and wait
For the Young Unknown.

IV

In the dark there careers –
As if Death astride came
To numb all with his knock –
A horse at mad rate
Over rut and stone.

V

No figure appears,
No call of my name,
No sound but "Tic–toc"
Without check. Past the gate
It clatters—is gone.

VI

What rider it bears
There is none to proclaim;
And the Old Year has struck,
And, scarce animate,
The New makes moan.

VII

    Maybe that "More Tears! –
    More Famine and Flame –
    More Severance and Shock!"
    Is the order from Fate
    That the Rider speeds on

To pale Europe; and tiredly the pines intone.

1915–1916.

"I MET A MAN"

I met a man when night was nigh,
Who said, with shining face and eye
Like Moses' after Sinai:—

"I have seen the Moulder of Monarchies,
Realms, peoples, plains and hills,
Sitting upon the sunlit seas! –
And, as He sat, soliloquies
Fell from Him like an antiphonic breeze
That pricks the waves to thrills.

"Meseemed that of the maimed and dead
Mown down upon the globe, –
Their plenteous blooms of promise shed
Ere fruiting–time—His words were said,
Sitting against the western web of red
Wrapt in His crimson robe.

"And I could catch them now and then:
—'Why let these gambling clans
Of human Cockers, pit liege men
From mart and city, dale and glen,

In death—mains, but to swell and swell again
      Their swollen All—Empery plans,

    '"When a mere nod (if my malign
      Compeer but passive keep)
Would mend that old mistake of mine
I made with Saul, and ever consign
All Lords of War whose sanctuaries enshrine
      Liberticide, to sleep?

    '"With violence the lands are spread
      Even as in Israel's day,
And it repenteth me I bred
Chartered armipotents lust—led
To feuds . . . Yea, grieves my heart, as then I said,
      To see their evil way!'

—"The utterance grew, and flapped like flame,
      And further speech I feared;
But no Celestial tongued acclaim,
And no huzzas from earthlings came,
And the heavens mutely masked as 'twere in shame
      Till daylight disappeared."

Thus ended he as night rode high –
The man of shining face and eye,
Like Moses' after Sinai.

1916.

174

"I LOOKED UP FROM MY WRITING"

I looked up from my writing,
　　And gave a start to see,
As if rapt in my inditing,
　　The moon's full gaze on me.

Her meditative misty head
　　Was spectral in its air,
And I involuntarily said,
　　"What are you doing there?"

"Oh, I've been scanning pond and hole
　　And waterway hereabout
For the body of one with a sunken soul
　　Who has put his life—light out.

"Did you hear his frenzied tattle?
　　It was sorrow for his son
Who is slain in brutish battle,
　　Though he has injured none.

"And now I am curious to look
　　Into the blinkered mind
Of one who wants to write a book
　　In a world of such a kind."

Her temper overwrought me,
　　And I edged to shun her view,
For I felt assured she thought me
　　One who should drown him too.

FINALE:

THE COMING OF THE END

How it came to an end!
The meeting afar from the crowd,
And the love–looks and laughters unpenned,
The parting when much was avowed,
How it came to an end!

It came to an end;
Yes, the outgazing over the stream,
With the sun on each serpentine bend,
Or, later, the luring moon–gleam;
It came to an end.

It came to an end,
The housebuilding, furnishing, planting,
As if there were ages to spend
In welcoming, feasting, and jaunting;
It came to an end.

It came to an end,
That journey of one day a week:
("It always goes on," said a friend,
"Just the same in bright weathers or bleak;")

176

But it came to an end.

    "HOW will come to an end
This orbit so smoothly begun,
Unless some convulsion attend?"
I often said. "What will be done
    When it comes to an end?"

    Well, it came to an end
Quite silently—stopped without jerk;
Better close no prevision could lend;
Working out as One planned it should work
    Ere it came to an end.

AFTERWARDS

When the Present has latched its postern behind my tremulous stay,
    And the May month flaps its glad green leaves like wings,
Delicate–filmed as new–spun silk, will the neighbours say,
    "He was a man who used to notice such things"?

If it be in the dusk when, like an eyelid's soundless blink,
    The dewfall–hawk comes crossing the shades to alight
Upon the wind–warped upland thorn, a gazer may think,
    "To him this must have been a familiar sight."

If I pass during some nocturnal blackness, mothy and warm,
    When the hedgehog travels furtively over the lawn,

Moments of Vision

One may say, "He strove that such innocent creatures should come to
no harm,
      But he could do little for them; and now he is gone"?

If, when hearing that I have been stilled at last, they stand at the
door,
      Watching the full–starred heavens that winter sees,
Will this thought rise on those who will meet my face no more,
      "He was one who had an eye for such mysteries"?

And will any say when my bell of quittance is heard in the gloom,
      And a crossing breeze cuts a pause in its outrollings,
Till they rise again, as they were a new bell's boom,
      "He hears it not now, but used to notice such things"?

Footnotes:

{1} Jer. li. 20.

Printed in the United States
68015LVS00004B/57